Que® Quick Reference Series

Harvard Graphics®
Quick Reference

Bryan Pfaffenberger

Que® Corporation
Carmel, Indiana

Harvard Graphics Quick Reference.

Library of Congress Catalog Number: 89-69832

ISBN 0-88022-538-6

92 91 90   4 3 2

Interpretation of the printing code: the rightmost double-digit number is the year of the book's printing; the rightmost single-digit number is the number of the book's printing. For example, a printing code of 89-4 shows that the fourth printing of the book occurred in 1989.

This book is based on Harvard Graphics Version 2.12.

Que Quick Reference Series

The *Que Quick Reference Series* is a portable resource of essential microcomputer knowledge. Whether you are a new or experienced user, you can rely on the high-quality information contained in these convenient guides.

Drawing on the experience of many of Que's best-selling authors, the *Que Quick Reference Series* helps you easily access important program information.

Now it's easy to look up often-used commands and functions for 1-2-3, dBASE IV, WordPerfect 5, Microsoft Word 5, and MS-DOS, as well as programming information for C, Turbo Pascal, and QuickBASIC 4.

Use the *Que Quick Reference Series* as a compact alternative to confusing and complicated traditional documentation.

The *Que Quick Reference Series* also includes these titles:

> *1-2-3 Quick Reference*
> *1-2-3 Release 2.2 Quick Reference*
> *1-2-3 Release 3 Quick Reference*
> *Assembly Language Quick Reference*
> *AutoCAD Quick Reference*
> *C Quick Reference*
> *dBASE IV Quick Reference*
> *DOS and BIOS Functions Quick Reference*
> *Hard Disk Quick Reference*
> *MS-DOS Quick Reference*
> *Microsoft Word 5 Quick Reference*
> *Norton Utilities Quick Reference*
> *PC Tools Quick Reference*
> *QuickBASIC Quick Reference*
> *Turbo Pascal Quick Reference*
> *WordPerfect Quick Reference*

Publishing Director
Lloyd J. Short

Product Director
Karen A. Bluestein

Editors
Shelley O'Hara
Cheryl Robinson

Technical Editor
Ron Holmes

Indexer
Joelynn Gifford

Production
Corinne Harmon
David Kline
Jennifer Matthews

Table of Contents

Introduction

Harvard Graphics Quick Reference includes the information you need as you create, edit, display, and print Harvard Graphics charts that range from simple to complex.

A reference guide of lasting value, this book is organized so that you easily can find the information you want. This book puts the information you need at your fingertips.

Harvard Graphics Quick Reference is divided into alphabetized sections by tasks, applications, and topics. One section, for instance, is called Linked Pie/Column Charts. Suppose that you want to link a pie chart with a column chart, but you cannot remember which option links the two charts. In such a situation, reach for this book to find a concise, clear explanation of what to do.

This book comprehensively sums up the knowledge you need to use Harvard Graphics effectively. This Quick Reference is not meant to take the place of a more comprehensive treatment of Harvard Graphics. This book assumes that you have a basic knowledge of the program.

If you want an introductory-level book that includes tutorials and information on good graphics practices, try Que Corporation's *Using Harvard Graphics*, by Stephen W. Sagman and Jane Graver Sandler.

Now you can put essential information at your fingertips with *Harvard Graphics Quick Reference*—and the entire Que Quick Reference series.

HINTS FOR USING THIS BOOK

Harvard Graphics Quick Reference is task-oriented—which means that it is oriented to *your* needs, not the structure of the program. Because topics are arranged alphabetically, begin with what *you* want to accomplish. For example, if you want information on how to use a film recorder, look under Film Recorder.

Within each section, subheadings help you find the information you need. For instance, some sections contain troubleshooting tips that help you solve common problems. Also, each section contains references to other sections that may help you as you create, edit, and print charts. All the graph chart options are listed under Graph Chart Options & Title Forms and all pie chart options are listed under Pie Chart Titles & Options.

Selecting Menu Options

You can choose options from menus and forms in the following ways:

- Press the up- and down- arrow keys.

Press either key until the option you want is selected.

- Press the first letter of an option.

Press the first letter of the menu option, such as **C** to select **C**reate new chart or **D** to choose **D**raw/Annotate. Within this book, the letter you type appears in **boldface blue** type. If two or more options begin with the same letter, press the letter more than once and then press **Enter**.

- Press the number or letter on the right margin of the menu.

Press this number or letter to select an option immediately. You do not need to press **Enter**.

- Press the space bar.

The space bar moves the highlight within the list. When the option you want is highlighted, press Enter.

To cancel a menu and return to the Main Menu, press Esc.

Using the Keyboard

You can use the cursor-movement keys and text editing keys in all or most situations. Some chart forms and program modes employ the keyboard in unique ways.

Cursor-Movement Keys

→	Moves one space right in text or one item right in menus.
Ctrl-→	Moves next word right in text.
←	Moves one space left in text or one item left in menus.
Ctrl-←	Moves to the previous word in text.
↑	Moves one line up in text or one item up in menus.
↓	Moves one line down in text or one item down in menus.
End	Moves to the last line on a text screen or the last item on a menu screen.
Home	Moves to the first line on a text screen or the first item on a menu screen.
Tab	Moves to the next line or item down.
Shift-Tab	Moves to the previous line or item.

Function Keys

Most Harvard Graphics' function key assignments change as you switch from one activity to another. You see the current function key options at the bottom of the screen. The following keys are almost always displayed:

F1 (Help)	Supplies information about the current screen.
F2 (Draw Chart)	Displays the Current Chart. Press **Esc** to return to the current screen.
F10 (Continue)	Same as pressing **Enter**.

You see these keys frequently in Chart Data and Options & Titles forms:

F3 (Set X Type)	In an area, bar/line, or high/low/close chart, displays the X Data Type Menu. (See X Axis Data Types.)
F4 (Calculate)	In an area, bar/line, or high/low/close chart, displays the Calculate window. (See Calculation.)
F4 (Redraw)	In Draw/Annotate, redraws entire chart in the chart box.
F4 (Spell Check)	When the Main Menu is displayed, starts Spell Check for the Current Chart. (See Spell Check.)
F5 (Attributes)	Controls text attributes such as fill, emphasis, and color. (See Attributes.)
Shift-F5	Selects entire line and displays Attributes menu. (See Attributes.)

F6	In Draw/Annotate, displays a menu of pattern and color choices when F8 (Options) is selected.
F6 (Colors)	In chart data forms, displays a menu of color attributes. (See Attributes.)
F7 (Size/Place)	Controls size and alignment of text. (See Size/Place.)
F8 (Options)	Displays Options and Titles forms for the current Chart Data form. After pressing F8 (Options), this key becomes F8 (Data). Press F8 (Data) to return to the Chart Data form.
F9 (More Series)	In an area, bar/line, or high/low/close chart, displays additional data series. Keep pressing this key to display the original data series.
F10 (Continue)	Selects the currently selected option or completes an operation and moves to the next screen.

Text Editing Keys

Del	Deletes the character on which the cursor is positioned.
Backspace	Deletes the character left of the cursor.
Ctrl-Ins	Inserts blank line at cursor.
Ctrl-Del	Deletes current line.

Using a Mouse

You can use any Microsoft or Microsoft-compatible mouse with Harvard Graphics. The mouse is especially useful when you use Draw/Annotate and Screenshows. Use the following techniques when you operate a mouse:

- To select an item from a menu, move the highlight to the option you want and click the left button.

- To select a function key, click both buttons. Then highlight the option you want at the bottom of the screen and press the left button.

- To page up and down in multi-page option forms, move the highlight off the top or bottom of the page.

- To remove a menu or screen as you do when you press Esc, click the right button.

The mouse has these special functions in Draw/ Annotate:

- To move the target, just move the mouse.

- Press the left button to duplicate the functions of the Enter key.

- Press the right button to duplicate the functions of the Esc key.

- Hold down the Shift key to force Harvard Graphics to draw a line horizontally or vertically, or to draw a square box.

When displaying a Screenshow, do the following:

- Press both mouse buttons to stop the show.

- Press the left mouse button to display the previous slide.

- Press the right mouse button to display the next slide.

COMMAND REFERENCE

Following is an alphabetical listing of task-oriented topics. Each entry covers the purpose, procedures, notes, and troubleshooting tips to quickly remind you of how to best use Harvard Graphics to create eye-catching charts and graphics.

Annotations

Purpose

Add text in different sizes, colors, and attributes to any Harvard Graphics chart you create. You are not limited as to where you can insert text, such as titles, subtitles, or footnotes.

Procedures

To add annotations or text to a chart:

1. Get the chart from disk.

2. Press Esc until you see the Main Menu.

3. Select Draw/Annotate.

4. Select Add.

5. Select Text.

6. Press F8 (Options) to change the size, color, emphasis, or alignment point.

7. Type the text in the box at the bottom of the screen.

   To set the attributes for a specific word or phrase, press F5 and select the attribute(s) you want.

8. Press Enter.

   The target is displayed on-screen.

9. Use the cursor-movement keys or the mouse to move the target where you want the text to appear.

10. Press **Enter** to confirm the text placement.

11. Press **Esc** until you return to the Main Menu.

12. Save your modified chart.

Options

Size	Enter a size from .5 through 100.
Color	Enter a number from 1 through 16.
Fill, Bold, Italic, Undrlin, Shadow	Press **Y** to select the attribute(s) you want.
Shadow Color	Press **F6** to select from a color list.
Align	Select the alignment point. The default alignment point is the center of the box's base.

Note

See also Attributes, Editing Objects, Copying an Object, and Deleting an Object.

Area Charts

Purpose

Use to show changes in volume. Area charts employ x- and y-axes. Generally, the x-axis categorizes or names the items, while the y-axis illustrates values.

Procedures

To create an area chart:

1. From the Main Menu, press **F8** to change the default orientation, border, and font settings for the chart.

2. Select **C**reate New Chart.

3. Select **A**rea.

4. When the X Data Type Menu appears, press the cursor-movement keys to choose a data type from the on-screen options. Select **N**ame and press **F10** to type the x-axis categories manually.

   If you want to enter calendrical, time, or numerical categories automatically, select **D**ay, **W**eek, **M**onth, **Q**uarter, **Y**ear, **M**onth/Day, **M**onth/Yr, or **Q**tr/Yr. Then press **Tab** to the Starting With field and type a starting date, time, or number. Type an ending date, time, or number at the Ending With field. You also can type an increment (the default is 1). Then press **F10** (Continue).

   If you see the message, `Error\: X data is invalid`, you entered the Starting With or Ending With information incorrectly.

5. At the Title field, type a title for your chart.

6. Move to the Subtitle field and type a subtitle, if you want.

7. Move to the Footnote field and type a footnote, if you want.

8. If you entered the x-axis category names automatically, the names appear in the next screen. If you chose **N**ame, tab to the x-axis column and type the first x-axis category name. Press **Enter** and type the second category name. Continue until you type all the x-axis category names.

9. Tab to the Series 1 column and type the y-axis values. You must enter numbers. You can use

scientific notation to enter very large or very small numbers. If the data you enter is larger than 10,000, Harvard Graphics automatically scales your data and places a legend (such as 'Thousands' or 'Millions') at the top left corner of the chart.

10. Tab to the Series 2 column and type the Series 2 data.

11. Continue adding additional series.

   You can enter up to a maximum of 8 data series in an area chart. To see the data columns for Series 5 through 8, press F9.

12. Press F2 (Draw Chart) to preview your chart.

13. Save the chart to disk.

Notes

You can change the following options on your Area Chart Titles & Options form (press F8).

To show y-axis values in a currency format, use the Y1 Axis Labels field (and the Y2 Axis Labels field, if you are using the Y2 Axis) on Page 3. Press Tab to move to the Format field (at the bottom of the same screen) and type ,2 under Y1 Axis or Y2 Axis.

To choose a three-dimensional effect, especially when you choose Overlap at the Chart Style field (Page 2), press Tab to the Chart Enhancement field and select 3d.

You can control the placement of x-axis labels with the X Axis Labels field on Page 3. You can align x-axis labels vertically instead of horizontally.

Add grid lines and control tick mark placement using the X Grid Lines, Y1 Grid Lines, Y2 Grid Lines, X Tick Mark Style, and Y Tick Mark Style fields on Page 3.

Change the attributes of the title, subtitle, x-axis, and y-axis labels with F5 (Attributes).

Perform calculations on data series and rows of data. Use series calculations to copy, exchange, move, and erase data series quickly.

Add visual appeal to your bar chart with symbols, freehand illustrations, and other enhancements using Draw/Annotate.

Keys

Use the following keystrokes to save time:

PgDn	Move to next page of Area Chart Titles & Options or Chart Data form.
PgUp	Move to previous page of Area Chart Titles & Options or Chart Data form.
Ctrl-Ins	In the Chart Data form, inserts a blank line in slice list to make room for a new data value.
Ctrl-Del	In the Chart Data form, deletes a line in the data value list or erases a title.
Ctrl-↑	In the Chart Data form, moves the current data value up in the list.
Ctrl-↓	In the Chart Data form, moves the current slice down in the list.

Troubleshooting Tips

If you encounter problems when you press **F2** (Draw), such as the values overlapping the labels, you can repair them from the Area Chart Titles & Options form.

- If your data includes one or two very large values and numerous small ones, the large areas are legible, but the smaller variations are illegible. You can highlight the variations among the smaller areas by choosing a logarithmic chart.

- If you choose **O**verlap at the Chart Style field in the Area Chart Titles & Options form and you cannot see one of the data series, place the smallest values in Series 1. Place the next larger values in Series 2, and so on.

- To reorder x-axis category names quickly, press **Ctrl-up arrow** and **Ctrl-down arrow** to move names up or down the list of x-axis values on the Area Chart Data form.

- If you have too many x-axis category names and
  they look squeezed together (or truncated), press F8
  (Options), select Yes at the Horizontal Chart field
  in the Area Chart Titles & Options form. If you do
  not want to see the chart horizontally, choose
  Vertical for x-axis labels.

- If you still have too many x-axis labels after
  displaying them vertically, reduce the number of
  x-axis labels you display. Type a minimum value
  and/or a maximum value in the X Axis column.
  You also can type an increment.

- If you created a chart with just one data series, you
  don't need the legend. In the Area Chart Titles &
  Options form, select None in the Legend Location
  field.

- If you create a chart with more than one data series
  and display legend, be sure to add legend titles. In
  the Area Chart Titles & Options form, type titles for
  each series you entered in the Legend Title field.

Notes

See also Attributes, Graph Charts Titles & Options
Form, Draw/Annotate, Currency Formats, Value
Formats, Calculations, Scaling, and X Axis Data Types.

Arrows and Lines

Purpose

Add arrows or lines to your chart by using Draw/
Annotate.

Procedures

To draw a line or arrow on your chart:

1. Display your chart and then press Esc until you
   see the Main Menu.

2. Select Draw/Annotate.

3. Select Add.

4. Select Line.

5. Press F8 (Options) to choose line options, if you want.

6. Press F8 (Draw) to draw the line or arrow.

7. Move the target to the point where you want the line or arrow to begin and press Enter.

8. Use the cursor-movement keys to move the target.

   Press Shift to force Harvard Graphics to draw the line vertically or horizontally.

9. Press Enter to complete the line or arrow.

10. Press Esc until you return to the Main Menu.

11. Save your chart.

Options

You can select from the following Line options:

Arrow	No arrow (default), arrow pointing left, arrow pointing right, two-headed arrow.
Width	Type a number from 1 to 100 to adjust the width of the line or arrow (default: 5.5).
Outline Draw	Select Yes (default) to draw an outline around the arrow. Choose No if you filled the center of the arrow with a distinctive color.
Outline Color	Press F6 (Choices) to choose colors from a menu.

Center Fill	Select Yes (default) to fill the line or arrow with the color indicated in Center Color. Select No to show the outline only.
Center Color	Press F6 (Choices) to choose colors from a menu.
Center Pattern	Press F6 (Choices) to see a menu of pattern choices. The default is 0 (no pattern).

Note

See also Editing Objects, Copying an Object, and Deleting an Object.

Attributes

Purpose

Add character enhancements to text in any Harvard Graphics chart, including italics, bold, and underline, as well as outline characters and the 16 standard Harvard Graphics colors.

Procedures

To change text attributes:

1. Display the Chart Data form if the text you want to change is a title, subtitle, axis label, or other chart text.

2. Move the cursor to the first character of the text you want to enhance.

3. Press F5 (Attributes) and use the cursor-movement keys to highlight the characters you want to change. Or, press Shift-F5 to highlight the whole line.

4. Press **Tab** and **Shift-Tab** to move from option to option in the Attributes menu at the bottom of the screen.

   Select Fill (if selected, the character is displayed and printed in a solid typeface; otherwise, the character appears in an outline typeface), Bold, Italic, Underline, and Color options.

5. To select or cancel an attribute, position the cursor on the attribute and press the space bar.

   Selected attributes are preceded by a pointer (a triangle).

6. Repeat Steps 4 and 5 to select or cancel additional attributes.

7. Press **F10** (Continue) to confirm your choices and assign the attributes to the text you selected.

To change the color of text:
1. Select the text you want to change.

2. Press **F5** to display the Attributes menu.

3. Press **Tab** to select the Color option.

4. Press **F6** (Colors).

5. Use the cursor-movement keys to choose a color.

6. Press **F10** (Continue).

═ Bar/Line Charts ═

Purpose
Use to create bar, line, and bar/line charts. Line charts are useful when you want to show trends in data over time. Use bar charts when you want to compare specific data points at intervals. Bar/line combination charts show changes in data over time while emphasizing a single factor or series.

Procedures

To create a bar/line chart:

1. At the Main Menu, press **F8** (Options) if you want to change the default orientation, border, and font settings for this chart.

2. Select Create New Chart.

3. Select Bar/Line.

4. When the X Data Type Menu appears, press the space bar to choose a data type.

   Select Name and press **F10** (Continue) if you want to type the x-axis categories manually.

   If you want to enter calendrical, time, or numerical categories automatically, select Day, Week, Month, Quarter, Year, Month/Day, Month/Yr, or Qtr/Yr. Type a starting date, time, or number in the Starting With field. Type an ending date, time, or number at the Ending With field. You also can type an increment (the default is 1). When you finish, press **F10** (Continue).

   If you see the message, `Error\: X data is invalid`, you entered the Starting With or Ending With information incorrectly.

5. At the Title field on the next page, type a title for your chart.

6. Tab to the Subtitle field and type a subtitle, if desired.

7. Tab to the Footnote field and type a footnote, if desired.

8. If you entered the x-axis category names automatically, the names already appear on-screen. If you chose Name, tab to the X axis column and type the first X axis category name. Press **Enter** to type the second category name. Continue until you type all the x-axis category names.

9. Tab to the Series 1 column and type the y-axis values.

You must enter numbers. You can use scientific notation to enter very large or very small numbers. If the data you enter are in figures larger than 10,000, Harvard Graphics automatically scales your data and places a legend (such as 'Thousands' or 'Millions') at the top left corner of the chart.

10. Tab to the Series 2 column and type the Series 2 data.

You can have up to 8 additional data series. To see the columns for Series 5 through 8, press F9.

11. Press F2 (Draw Chart) to preview your chart.

12. Save the chart to disk.

Keys

Use the following keystrokes to save time:

PgDn	Moves to the next page of Bar/Line Chart Titles & Options form or Chart Data form.
PgUp	Moves to the previous page of Bar/Line Chart Titles and Options form or Chart Data form.
Ctrl-Ins	In the Chart Data form, inserts a blank line in slice list to make room for a new data value.
Ctrl-Del	In the Chart Data form, deletes a line in the data value list or erases a title.
Ctrl-↑	In the Chart Data form, moves the current data value up in the list.
Ctrl-↓	In the Chart Data form, moves the current slice down in the list.

Troubleshooting Tips

If you encounter problems when you press F2 (Draw), such as the values overlapping the labels, repair errors using the Bar/Line Chart Titles & Options form. Make note of the following problem solving strategies:

- If your data includes one or two large values and numerous small ones, the large bars are legible while the smaller variations are illegible. Highlight the variations among the smaller areas by choosing a logarithmic chart.

- If you want to show more than one data series and the bars are too thin, press **Tab** to move to Bar Style and choose **O**verlap.

- To reorder x-axis category names quickly on the Bar/Line Chart Data form, press **Ctrl-↑** and **Ctrl-↓**.

- If the x-axis category names look squeezed together (or truncated), press **Tab** to move to Horizontal Chart in the Bar/Line Chart Titles & Options form and choose **Y**es. If you do not want a horizontal chart, move to X Axis Labels and choose **V**ertical.

- If you created a chart with just one data series, you can delete the legend. In the Bar/Line Chart Titles & Options form, move to Legend Location and choose **N**one.

- If you create a chart with more than one data series, make sure that you add legend titles.

Notes

The Bar/Line Chart Titles & Options form lists many options for displaying your bar chart. The following discussion is a quick overview of commonly used options.

To display y-axis values in a currency format, use the Y1 Axis Labels field (and the Y2 Axis Labels field, if you are using the Y2 Axis). Then move to the Format field (at the bottom of the same screen) and type **,2** under the Y1 Axis or Y2 Axis column.

Create a combination bar/line chart by moving to the Scale Type field and choosing display options for each series independently.

For Bar Enhancement, select **3**d to show a three-dimensional effect.

Control the display of the legend by specifying Legend Location, Legend Justify, Legend Placement, and Legend Frame in the appropriate fields.

Control the placement of x-axis labels using the X Axis Labels field. You can align x-axis labels vertically instead of horizontally.

Add grid lines and control tick mark placement using the X Grid Lines, Y1 Grid Lines, Y2 Grid Lines, X Tick Mark Style, and Y Tick Mark Style fields.

You can change the attributes of the chart title, subtitle, and footnote.

Show currency formats in foreign currencies.

Choose values formats to control the display of y-axis values.

Perform calculations on data series and rows of data. Use series calculations to copy, exchange, move, and erase data series quickly.

Add visual appeal to your bar chart with symbols, freehand illustrations, and other enhancements using Draw/Annotate.

See also Combination Charts, Cumulative Charts, Dual Y-Axis Charts, Line Charts, Logarithmic Charts, Normalized (100%) Charts, Paired Bar Charts, Point Charts, Stacked Bar Charts, Trend Line Charts, Graph Chart Titles & Options Forms, X-Axis Data Types, Attributes, Draw/Annotate, Currency Formats, Values Formats, and Calculations.

Borders

Purpose

Harvard Graphics is preset to print your charts without a border. You can change this default setting so that your charts print with a single-width or double-width border. You also can override the default setting temporarily so that only the current chart is affected.

Procedures

To set a new default border:

1. From the Main Menu, select **S**etup.

2. Select **D**efaults.

3. Use the **Tab** key, the cursor-movement keys, or the mouse to select the Border option.

4. Press the space bar to choose **N**one, **S**ingle, or **D**ouble.

5. Press **Enter**.

   Harvard Graphics saves the option you chose, and that option becomes the new default.

To override the default border choice temporarily:

1. Press **F8** (Options) when the Main Menu is displayed.

2. Use the **Tab** key, the cursor-movement keys, or the mouse to select the Border option.

3. Select the border you want: **N**one, **S**ingle, or **D**ouble.

Note

See also Boxes.

Boxes

Purpose

Use Draw/Annotate to add a box to your chart. You can select the outline style, and you can fill the box with a color or pattern.

Procedure

To add a box to your chart:

1. With the chart on-screen, press **Esc** until you see the Main Menu.

2. Select **D**raw/Annotate.

3. Select **A**dd.

4. Select **B**ox.

5. Press **F8** (Options) to select the options you want.

6. Press **F8** (Draw) to resume drawing after you choose the options.

7. Position the target where you want the box's upper left corner to appear.

   Press the grey - and grey + keys to change the cursor-movement increment.

8. Press **Enter** to anchor the upper left corner.

9. Position the target where you want the box's lower right corner to appear.

   To constrain Harvard Graphics to draw a symmetrical box, hold down the **Shift** key as you move the cursor.

10. Press **Enter** to anchor the lower right corner.

Options

You can use the following Box options:

Square	Select **Y**es to force Harvard Graphics to draw a square. The default is **N**o.
Style	Select from the following:

1 **P**lain—the default style. A box with single-width lines.

2 **F**rame—double box.

3 **O**ctagonal frame—double box with rounded edges.

4 **R**ounded—a box with single-width lines and rounded edges.

5 **O**ctagonal—a box with single-width lines and bevelled edges.

6—plain box with shadow right and bottom.

7—plain box with shadow top and right.

8—plain box with shadow top and left.

9—plain box with shadow bottom and left.

10—plain box with 3-D effect right and bottom.

11—plain box with 3-D effect top and right.

12—plain box with 3-D effect top and left.

13—plain box with 3-D effect bottom and left.

14—page with bottom right corner upturned.

15—page with top right corner upturned.

16—page with top left corner upturned.

17—page with bottom left corner upturned.

18—caption with arrow pointing down.

19—caption with arrow pointing right.

20—caption with arrow pointing up.

21—caption with arrow pointing left.

Size   Type a different box size for special effects, such as the width of the frame in Styles 2 and 3, the width of the shadow in Styles 6 through 9, and the width of the upturned page in Styles 14 through 17. The default is 5.5.

Outline Draw	Select **N**o to omit the outline around the box, showing only the color you chose to fill the box. The default is **Y**es.
Outline Color	Press **F6** (Choices) to see a palette of color options. The default setting depends on your hardware.
Center Fill	With the default **Y**es, the box is filled with the color indicated in Center Color or the pattern chosen in Center Pattern. Select **N**o to draw a box outline only.
Center Color	Default color depends on your hardware. Press **F6** (Choices) to see a palette of color options.
Center Pattern	Press **F6** (Choices) to see a menu of pattern choices. The default is 0 (no pattern).
Center Shadow Color	Default color depends on your hardware. Press **F6** (Choices) to see a menu of color options.

Note

See also Editing Objects, Copying an Object, and Deleting an Object.

Bullet Lists

Purpose

Adds a symbol, such as a dot, a hyphen, a check mark, or a square, before a series. Use to communicate a series of ideas or list a set of items.

The default bullet character is a dot. You can override the default if you want. You also can add space between the bullet and the text, create an outline effect by adding indented subentries (which are also bulleted), and change the color of the bullet.

Procedures

To create a bullet list text chart:

1. At the Main Menu, press **F8** (Options) if you want to change the default orientation, border, and font settings for this chart.

2. Select Create New Chart.

3. Select Text.

4. Select Bullet List.

5. At the Title field, type a title for the chart.

6. Press **Tab** to move to the Subtitle field, and type a subtitle.

   Because a Subtitle is optional, press **Tab** to skip it.

7. Press **Tab** to move to the Footnote field.

   You can choose to skip the Footnote field by pressing **Tab**.

8. Press **Tab** to move to the bullet list area.

9. Type the first item you want in the list.

10. Press **Enter** twice.

11. Type the next item you want in the list.

12. Repeat Steps 10 and 11 to complete the chart.

13. Press **F2** (Draw Chart) to preview the chart on-screen.

    If some lines overflow the screen, correct the problem by using the Size/Place command.

14. Save the chart to disk.

To change a bullet:

1. With the Bullet List text screen displayed, press **F7** to select the Size/Place command.

2. Use the arrow keys to select the bullet place. Press the space bar to select a new bullet character.

3. Press **F10** (Continue).

To indent text after a bullet:

1. Place the cursor on the line you want to indent.

2. Press **F7** (Size/Place).

3. Use the cursor-movement keys to highlight the L(eft) option and press the space bar if the option is not already selected. You see a pointer next to the L when you select the flush left alignment.

4. Press the **Tab** key to highlight the Indent option.

5. Type a number between 1 and 99.

   The number refers to a percent of the width of the chart or screen. To position the beginning of the line at the center of the chart, for example, type **50**

6. Press **F10** (Continue).

To create an outline effect by adding indented subentries:

1. Type the first bulleted heading.

2. Press **Enter**

3. Press **Ctrl-B**. Use the cursor-movement keys to select the bullet you want for the second-level heading. Press **Enter**

4. Press the **space bar** and type the second-level heading.

5. Repeat Steps 3 and 4 to type additional second-level headings.

6. When you finish typing second-level headings, press **Enter** twice to begin a main-level heading.

Notes

You can change the attributes of any on-screen text.

Add visual appeal to your bulleted list with symbols, freehand illustrations, and other enhancements using Draw/Annotate.

After you complete your chart, perform a spell check.

See also Attributes, Size/Place, Draw/Annotate, and Spell Check.

Bullets

Purpose

Adds a symbol, such as a dot or hyphen, to mark items in a list in any text chart, even if you did not choose the Bullet List option in the Text Chart Styles menu.

Procedures

To insert a bullet:

1. Position the cursor where you want the bullet to appear.

2. Press **Ctrl-B**.

3. Use the **space bar** to select the bullet symbol you want.

4. Press **Enter** to place the bullet on your chart.

To remove a bullet:

Delete the bullet character as you delete any unwanted character.

To change the color of a bullet:

1. Insert a blank space after the bullet.

2. Press **F5** (Attributes) and select the color you want.

3. Press **F10** (Continue).

Note

See also Attributes.

Calculation

Purpose

Analyzes data you entered and inserts the results in a
new data series on any Bar/Line chart, Area, chart, or
High/Low/Close chart. The results are then graphically
displayed in a format you choose.

You can perform calculations two ways:

- *Row calculations* perform operations across two or
  more data series. If you enter data on the sales of
  Model A in Series 1 and Model B in Series 2 for the
  month of January, for instance, you can sum the
  two to show the total sales for January. Harvard
  Graphics places the sum in Series 3.

- *Series calculations* perform operations on a single
  data series. If you enter data on the sales of Model
  A for all the months of the year in Series 1, for
  instance, you can generate a running cumulative
  total. Harvard Graphics places the cumulative total
  figures in Series 2.

Use row calculations to find sums, averages, maximum
figures, and minimum figures. Use series calculations to
calculate cumulative totals, moving averages, and
statistical trends. Use series calculations to edit data
series quickly. You can erase a series, copy a series,
move a series, and exchange one series with another.

Procedure

To perform a calculation and create a new data series:

1. Display the Chart Data form of your bar/line,
   area, or high/low/close chart.

2. Position the cursor at the top of a blank data
   series.

   When Harvard Graphics places the results in the
   data series where the cursor is located. If you
   place the cursor in a data series that already
   contains data, the program overwrites the data.

If you do not see any blank data series, press **F9** (More Series).

3. Press **F4** (Calculate).

4. When the Calculate window appears, type the number of a blank series if you did not place the cursor in a blank series (as described in Step 2).

5. Move to the Legend field and type a series legend title.

6. Enter the calculation instruction.

To tell Harvard Graphics how to perform the calculations, carefully follow these calculation syntax rules:

- Refer to data series using a pound sign (#). For example, to refer to Series 2, type **#2**

- Use symbols to refer to addition (+), subtraction (-), multiplication (*), and division (/). For example, to tell Harvard Graphics to multiply Series 2 by 1.672 and place the results in a new series, type **#2 * 1.672**

Important: The order of calculation is strictly left to right. You cannot use parentheses to override the order of calculation.

Use keywords to perform calculations on several series or on rows of data across series.

You can use row keywords or series keywords. When you use row keywords, you can name more than one data series. Separate the data series using commas, as in the following example:

@SUM(#1,#2,#3)

You can name only one data series when you use series keywords, such as

@MAVG(#4)

7. Press **Enter**.

If you see the message Error: Improper Calculation
Syntax, make sure that you spelled the keyword
correctly and preceded each series reference with a
pound sign (#). Series references must be enclosed in
parentheses. Press **F4** (Calculate) and type the
instruction again.

Notes

Harvard Graphics does not employ automatic
recalculation. If you create a calculated series that draws
on data from another series, the calculated series may
not be correct if you do not use the command that
recalculates the data. For example, suppose that Series 2
contains a moving average of the data in Series 1, but
you changed one of the Series 1 data points. Series 2
will not contain the correct data until you use the
@RECALC keyword.

For a list of keywords, see Keywords.

═ **Chartbooks**

Purpose

Holds the templates you create. A chartbook is a
collection of templates stored on disk. Note that you
must create templates before you create a chartbook.

Procedures

To create a chartbook:

1. From the Main Menu., select Chartbook Menu.

2. Select Create Chartbook.

3. At the Directory field, type the name of the DOS
   directory in which you want to store the
   chartbook.

4. At the Chartbook Name field, type a name for
   the chartbook.

This name must conform to the DOS convention of up to eight letters or numbers, but do not type a period or extension.

5. Press Tab and type a description of the chartbook.

6. Press Enter

   You see a screen showing the current templates on the top half of the screen. You select templates from this list so that they appear in the bottom half of the screen, which shows the chartbook contents when you finish.

7. Use the up- or down-arrow keys to select a template in the top half of the screen. Then press Enter to add the template to the chartbook.

   Press Tab to move between the top and bottom window.

8. Repeat Step 7 until you add all the templates you want to include in the chartbook.

9. Press F10 to save the chartbook to disk.

To edit a chartbook:

1. From the Main Menu, select Chartbook.

2. Choose Select Chartbook.

3. Press the up- or down-arrow keys to choose the chartbook from the list.

   Press F3 (Change Dir) if you do not see the chartbook on the list.

4. Press Esc to return to the Chartbook Menu.

5. Select Edit Chartbook.

6. When you see the Create/Edit Chartbook screen, you can perform the following operations:

   • Reorganize the template list by placing the cursor on a template name in the bottom window and pressing Ctrl-up arrow or Ctrl-down arrow

- Add a template to the chartbook by placing the cursor on a template name in the top window and pressing Enter.

  - Delete a template from the chartbook by placing the cursor on the template name and pressing Ctrl-Del..

7. Press Tab to move between the top and bottom window.

8. Press F10 (Continue) when you finish editing the chartbook.

Note

See also Templates.

Circles and Ellipses

Purpose

Use Draw/Annotate to add circles and ellipses to your chart.

Procedures

To draw a circle:

1. With the chart displayed, press Esc until you see the Main Menu.

2. Select Draw/Annotate.

3. Select Add.

4. Select Circle.

5. Press F8 (Options) to choose Circle Options.

   By default, Harvard Graphics draws a circle. If you want to draw an ellipse, you must use the Circle Options menu and then select the Ellipse option at the Shape field.

6. Press **F8** (Draw) to draw the circle or ellipse.

7. Move the target to the center of the circle or ellipse and press **Enter**.

8. Use the cursor-movement keys to move the target.

   You see a box that shows the extent of the circle or ellipse that Harvard Graphics will insert.

9. Press **Enter** to complete the circle or ellipse.

10. Press **Esc** to return to the Add menu.

Options

Use the following Circle options:

Shape	The default is **C**ircle. Choose **E**llipse to draw an oval.
Outline Draw	The default draws an outline around the circle or ellipse. Choose **N**o if you filled the center of the arrow with a distinctive color.
Outline Color	The default color depends on your hardware. Press **F6** (Choices) to select colors from a menu.
Center Fill	Keep the default, **Y**es, to fill the circle or ellipse with the color indicated in Center Color. Choose **N**o to show the outline only.
Center Color	The default color depends on your hardware. Press **F6** (Choices) to select colors from a menu.

Center Pattern   Press F6 (Choices) to see a
                        menu of pattern choices. The
                        default is 0 (no pattern).

Note

See also Editing Objects, Copying an Object, and
Deleting an Object.

Column Charts

Purpose

Similar to a pie chart. Shows the values as parts of a
whole. You follow the same steps you take to create a
pie chart, but you choose an option that displays the data
as a column rather than a pie chart.

Procedures

To create a column chart:

1. Follow the instructions for pie charts to enter the
   chart title, subtitle, footnote, and data.

2. Press F8 (Options).

3. Press PgDn to move to Page 2 of Pie Chart
   Titles & Options form.

4. Move to the Chart Style field and select Column
   under Pie 1. Then press F8 (Data) to return to the
   Pie Chart Data form.

4. Press F2 to preview your chart.

5. Save the chart to disk.

To scale column chart values and add a legend:

Harvard Graphics does not automatically scale
column chart values. If you create a column chart
with large values, you must scale the values and add
a legend manually.

To *scale* values means to reduce them by a common factor, such as 100 or 1000, reducing the length of values and reduce the visual complexity of the chart. For instance, if your chart shows sales of a product in the range $100,000 to $700,000, you can scale the graph by a factor of 1,000.

The chart will display the values divided by 1,000 ($100 and $700). Always add a legend, such as 'Hundreds' or 'Thousands' so that your audience understands the scaling factor.

1. Press **F8** (Options).

2. Press **PgDn** to show Page 2 of the Pie Chart Titles & Options form.

3. Move to the Value Formats option.

4. Type **100** or **1000** followed by a vertical line character (|).

   To specify how many decimal places Harvard Graphics will display, type the number of decimal places after the vertical line character (**1000|2** displays the value in thousands with two decimal places).

5. Press **F2** (Draw) to preview the formatting.

6. Press **Esc** to return to Page 2 of the Pie Chart Titles & Options form.

7. Press **PgUp** to show Page 1 of the Pie Chart Titles & Options form.

8. Type the scaling factor (such as hundreds or thousands) at the Footnote field or Pie 1 Title field.

   You can control the size and alignment of this legend by pressing **F7** (Size/Place).

9. Press **F2** (Draw) to preview the legend.

10. Save your chart.

Notes

The Pie Chart Titles & Options form lists many options for displaying your column chart. The following is an overview of commonly used options:

- To display the columns in order of magnitude (rather than the order you typed them), tab to the Sort Slices field and select **Y**es.

- To display values in currency, tab to the Currency field, and select **Y**es. Then tab to the Value Format field and type **,2** (a comma followed by the number 2).

- To display percentages next to each value, tab to the Show Percent field and select **Y**es. Tab to the Place Percent field and select **A**djacent so that the percentages do not interfere with the labels and values.

- To display the column with a three-dimensional effect, tab to the 3D Effect field and select **Y**es.

- To change the attributes of the chart title, subtitle, and footnote, press **F5** (Attributes).

To add visual appeal to your column chart with symbols, freehand illustrations, and other enhancements, use Draw/Annotate.

Troubleshooting Tips

If you encounter problems when you press **F2** (Draw), such as the values overlapping the labels, use the many options available in the Pie Chart Titles & Options form to correct the errors. Here's a quick overview of problem-solving strategies:

- **Tab** to the Place Value field and choose **A**djacent to display the values next to the labels so that they don't overlap.

- If the column is too large or too small, tab to the Pie Size field and type a slightly larger or smaller number.

- If the labels are too large or some labels are truncated, reduce the type size by typing a smaller number at the Label Size field.

See also Attributes, Draw/Annotate, Pie Charts, Pie Chart Titles & Options Form, Scaling, and Value Formats.

Column Text Charts

Purpose

Column text charts show lists of related items side-by-side in a two- or three-column format. For instance, you can use a two-column text chart to list advantages and disadvantages. You can use a three-column text chart to list revenues over a three-month period.

Procedures

To create a column text chart:

1. At the Main Menu, press **F8** (Options) if you want to change the default orientation, border, and font settings for this chart.

2. Select Create New Chart.

3. Select Text.

4. Select Two Columns or Three Columns.

5. Type a title for the chart in the Title field.

6. Press **Tab** to move to the Subtitle field and type a subtitle.

   The subtitle is optional. To skip it, just press **Tab**

7. Press **Tab** to move to the Footnote field.

   The footnote is also optional. To skip it, just press **Tab**.

8. Press **Tab** to move to the first column title box.

9. Type the title.

10. Press **Tab** to move to the first column header box, and type the title of the first column.

11. Press **Tab** to move to the second column header box, and type the title of the second column.

    If you are creating a three-column chart, press **Tab** and type the third column's title.

12. Press **Tab** to move to the first column and type an item.

    If you are typing a number, Harvard Graphics right-aligns the item. (A number can include the a dollar sign and commas.) If you are typing any other text, it is aligned automatically on the left.

13. Press **Tab** to move to the second column and type an item.

    If you are creating a three-column chart, press **Tab** and type the third column's item.

14. Repeat Steps 12 and 13 until the text chart is completed.

15. Press **F2** (Draw Chart) to preview the chart on-screen.

    If some of the lines overflow the screen, correct the problem by using the Size/Place command.

16. Save the chart to disk.

To change the spacing between columns:

1. Press **F7** (Size/Place).

2. Press **Tab** to go to the Column Spacing field.

3. Select from the S(mall), M(edium), (L)arge, and e(X)tra large options.

4. Press **F2** (Draw Chart) to see how much space Harvard Graphics inserted between columns.

Notes

You can change the attributes of any text on the screen.

Add visual appeal to your pie chart with symbols, freehand illustrations, and other enhancements using Draw/Annotate.

After you complete your chart, perform a spell check.

See also Attributes, Draw/Annotate, Size/Place, and Spell Check.

Combination Charts

Purpose

Shows two or more data series in different ways. You can display one data series with bars, and use lines for another. You also can show one or more data series as an area chart and combine this display with lines or bars. If you created a high/low/close chart, you can add additional data series and display them with lines or bars.

You create a bar/line combination chart by following the instructions for bar/line charts. To create a combination chart that includes a data series displayed as an area chart, follow the instructions for area charts. To create a high/low/close combination chart, you begin by following the instructions for high/low/close charts. Before you begin, decide which data series you want to show with bars and which you want to show with lines.

Procedures

To create a bar/line or area combination chart:

1. Follow the instructions for bar/line charts or for area charts (depending on the type of chart you are creating).

2. Press F8 (Options).

3. On Page 1 of the Bar/Line Chart or Area Chart Titles & Options form, press **Tab** to move to the table at the bottom of the screen that contains the series legend titles.

4. Place the cursor on the Series 1 field and press **Tab**.

5. Select **B**ar, **L**ine, **T**rend, or **C**urve for bar/line combination chart. Select **A**rea, **B**ar, **L**ine, or **T**rend for any combination chart, including an area chart data series.

6. Repeat Steps 4 and 5 for additional data series.

7. Press **PgDn** to see Page 4 of the Bar/Line Chart or Area Chart Titles & Options form.

8. Press **Tab** to go to the table at the bottom of the screen that contains the series legend titles.

9. Place the cursor on the first data series you defined.

10. Press **Tab** to go to the Marker/Pattern column and select a different marker pattern, if you want.

    Choose from 13 marker patterns: **0**—none, **1**—dot, **2**—plus, **3**—asterisk, **4**—square, **5**—x, **6**—diamond, **7**—up triangle, **8**—partially boxed X, **9**—circle, **10**—down triangle, **11**—star, **12**—boxed X, **13**—outline plus.

11. Press **Tab** to go to the Line Style column and choose a different line style.

    You can choose from 4 line styles: **1**—thin, **2**—thick, **3**—dotted, and **4**—dashed.

12. Repeat Steps 9 through 11 for additional data series.

13. Press **F2** (Draw Chart) to preview your chart.

14. Save the chart to disk.

To create a combination high/low/close and bar/line chart:

1. Display your high/low/close chart and press **F9** (More Series).

2. Add additional data in Series 5.

   You also can add data to Series 6, 7, and 8, if you want.

3. Press F8 (Options) to see the Series 5, 6, 7, or 8 data in a format other than line.

   Press Tab to go to the Type option and select Bar, Trend, Curve, or Pt.

Notes

Use calculations to determine the daily average value and place the average in Series 5.

See also Area Charts, Bar/Line Charts, and High/Low/Close Charts.

Copying an Object

Purpose

After you create an object, you can copy the object to other places on your chart.

Procedures

To copy an object:

1. Display the chart with the object.

2. Press Esc to return to the Main Menu.

3. Select Draw/Annotate.

4. Select Copy.

5. Place the target on the object you want to copy and press Enter.

6. Select Choose This.

7. Move the target to where you want the copy of the object to appear and press Enter.

You can make multiple copies by moving the target again and pressing Enter

8. Press Esc to return to the Main Menu and save your modified chart.

Creating New Charts

Purpose

You can choose to create any number of different charts. For specific directions, look up the type of chart you want to create.

Notes

See also Area Chart, Bar/Line Chart, Bullet List, Column Chart, Column Text Chart, Combination Chart, Cumulative Chart, Dual Y Axis Chart, Free Form Text Chart, High/Low/Close Chart, Linked Pie/Column Chart, Logarithmic Chart, Normalized (100%) Chart, Organization Chart, Paired Bar Chart, Pie Chart, Point Chart, Simple List Chart, Stacked Bar Chart, Text Chart, Title Chart, Trend Line Chart, Two Pie/Column Chart.

Cumulative Charts

Purpose

Shows data as a running total. Each data point represents the sum of previous data points, beginning with the first data point in the series.

You create a cumulative chart by following the instructions for bar/line charts or area charts. Then you press F8 (Options) to define the chart as a cumulative chart.

Procedures

To create a cumulative chart:

1. Follow the instructions for Bar/Line Charts or Area Charts to enter initial data.

2. Press F8 (Options).

3. Press PgDn to display Page 4 of the Bar/Line Chart Titles & Options form.

4. Press Tab to go to the table at the bottom of the screen that contains the series legend titles.

5. Place the cursor on the first data series.

6. Press Tab and choose Yes in the Cum(ulative) column.

7. Repeat Steps 5 and 6 for additional data series.

8. Press F2 (Draw Chart) to preview your chart.

9. Save the chart to disk.

Note

See also Area Charts, Bar/Line Chart, and X Axis Data Types.

Current Chart

Purpose

After you create a chart or retrieve one from disk, it remains in memory even after you press Esc to return to the Main Menu. From the Main Menu, you can print the current chart, add annotations using Draw/Annotate, or save the chart. To edit the current chart, select Enter/Edit chart from the Main Menu.

Procedures

To choose current chart options:

1. With the Main Menu displayed, press F8 (Options).

If you do not see the Main Menu, press Esc

2. To select an Orientation option, press the space bar to select Landscape or Portrait.

   Skip this step if you want to leave the Orientation setting as it is.

3. Press Enter to move to the Border options.

4. Press the space bar to choose a Border option: None, Single, or Double.

   Skip this step if you want to leave the Border setting as it is.

5. Press Enter to move to the Font options.

6. Press the space bar to select a Font option: Executive, Square, Serif, Roman, Sans Serif, Script, or Gothic.

7. Press F10 (Continue) to save your choices and return to the Main Menu.

Notes

If you select Create New Chart from the Main Menu and a chart is still in memory, you see a warning.

If you are changing from one type of graph to another (for instance, from a text chart to a graph chart), you see a warning message informing you that your work will be lost. Press Enter to abandon your work or Esc to cancel.

If you are changing to a different chart type within the general chart type (text, pie, organization, or graph chart), you see the Change Chart Type menu. You can retain the data from the current chart. Select Yes to keep the data or No to abandon it.

Use the Current Chart Options to override the orientation, border, and font settings for the current chart.

See also Border, Font, and Orientation.

Data Reduction

Purpose

Use to resort the x-axis when the values are out of order or contain duplicates for some reason. Data reduction is rarely necessary, but may prove useful if you use imported data.

When you use data reduction, Harvard Graphics performs the following operations:

- Examines all x- and y-values to make sure that they are valid entries.

- If there are two y-values in a series for one x-axis label, the program sums the values.

- If you chose the Number data type for your x-axis labels, Harvard Graphics does not sum duplicate values.

- Sorts the x-axis labels and rearranges the y-axis data accordingly.

- The program does not sort x-axis labels if you chose the Name data type.

- If the program encounters any y-values that do not have x-axis labels, these values are placed after the sorted data.

Procedures

To reduce data automatically:

1. Display the Chart Data form for the bar/line, area, or high/low/close chart you created.

2. Press F4 (Calculate).

3. When the Calculate window appears, press Tab to go to the Calculation option and type @REDUC

4. Press Enter.

Note

See also X Axis Data Types.

Default Settings

Purpose

Most application programs come to you preset for a
"plain vanilla" hardware environment. Harvard Graphics
uses the following preset or default settings, which it
uses unless you specifically instruct the program
otherwise:

Chart Options	Landscape orientation, no border, Executive font.
Film Recorder	Polaroid Palette connected via serial port COM1.
Plotter	HP ColorPro plotter connected via serial port COM1 (settings: 9600 baud, 8 data bits, 1 stop bit, no parity).
Printer	IBM Graphics Printer connected via parallel port LPT1.
Screen	Harvard Graphics automatically determines the proper setting for your system during installation.

Note

See also Installing Harvard Graphics, Setup Options,
Film Recorders, Plotters, and Printers.

Deleting an Object

Purpose

Deletes an object from your chart.

Procedures

To delete an object:

1. Display the chart with the object.

2. Press Esc to return to the Main Menu.

3. Select Draw/Annotate.

4. Select Delete.

5. Select Choose.

6. Move the target to the item you want to delete and press Enter

7. Select Choose This and press Enter

8. Press Esc to return to the Main Menu and save your modified chart.

To delete all objects:

1. Display the chart with the objects.

2. Press Esc to return to the Main Menu.

3. Select Draw/Annotate.

4. Select Delete.

5. Select All.

6. In response to the `Delete all drawings?` prompt, press Enter

7. Press Esc to return to the Main Menu and save your modified chart.

Note

If you delete one object, you can select Undo from the Delete menu to undo the deletion. But if you select All and delete all objects, you cannot undo the deletion.

Draw/Annotate

Purpose

Enables you to add lines, boxes, circles, polygons,
polylines, text, and symbols to charts.

Keys

Use the following keys with Draw/Annotate:

↑	Moves up.
PgUp	Moves diagonally up and right.
→	Moves right.
PgDn	Moves diagonally down and right.
↓	Moves down.
End	Moves diagonally down and left.
←	Moves left.
Home	Moves diagonally up and left.
Ctrl-Up	Moves to top margin of chart box.
Ctrl-PgUp	Moves to upper right corner of chart box.
Ctrl-→	Moves to right margin of chart box.
Ctrl-PgDn	Moves to lower right corner of chart box.
Ctrl-↓	Moves to bottom margin of chart box.

Ctrl-End	Moves to lower left corner of chart box.
Ctrl-←	Moves to left margin of chart box.
Ctrl-Home	Moves to upper left corner of chart box.
keypad +	Increases the amount of cursor movement.
keypad -	Decreases the amount of cursor movement.
keypad *	Restores the default amount of cursor movement.

Note

See also Annotations, Arrows, Boxes, Circles, Polygons, Polylines, and Symbols. You also can edit the drawings you create. See Editing Objects, Copying an Object, and Deleting an Object.

Draw Chart

Purpose

Use to cycle between viewing your chart and making modifications.

Procedures

To view the chart:

Press F2 (Draw Chart) at any time after you enter your data.

To return to the chart definition screen:

Press Esc.

Dual Y Axis Charts

Purpose

Use to compare two data series that require different
y-axis scales. You can show the relationship between
two data series that are measured differently. Because
Harvard Graphics can display two y-axes, Y1 (left side
of chart) and Y2 (right), you easily can create a dual
y-axis chart.

Procedures

To create a dual y-axis chart:

1. Follow the instructions for bar/line charts to
   create your chart and enter the data.

   To avoid confusion, limit your chart to two data
   series.

2. Press F8 (Options).

3. Press Tab to go to the Y1 Axis Title field and
   type a title.

   Type a title that describes the measurement used
   for Series 1.

4. Press Tab to go to the Y2 Axis Title field and
   type a title.

   Type a title that describes the measurement used
   for Series 2.

5. Press Tab to go to Series 2 under the Legend
   Title column and tab over to the Y-axis column.

6. Select Y2.

7. Press F2 (Draw Chart) to display the chart.

Note

See also Bar/Line Charts.

Editing Charts

Purpose

Use to make changes or to change the chart style.

In some cases, you can change the style without losing the data values, titles, and other information you typed. In general, you can change pie charts into area, bar/line, or high/low/close charts, and you can change any of these charts into pie charts (when you have only one or two data series). You cannot change text charts or organization charts into another chart style.

Procedures

To edit a chart you created:

1. Retrieve the chart from disk.

2. Display the Chart Data form.

3. Press F8 (Options) to change the options and titles.

4. Make any changes.

5. Save the chart to disk.

To change the chart style:

1. Specify the chart you want to change as the current chart.

2. From the Main Menu, select Create New Chart.

3. When you see the message, Keep current data, choose Yes.

Notes

If you included a chart in a chartbook or multiple chart, Harvard Graphics automatically uses the most recent version of the chart should you make changes to it.

See also Spell Check.

Editing Objects

Purpose

After you use Draw/Annotate to add an object—
annotations, arrows, boxes, circles, polygons, and
polylines—you can change its options, move it, or resize
it. You choose the editing option you want from the
Draw menu, select the object or objects you want to
modify, and proceed with the editing operation.

Procedures

To move an object:

1. Display the chart with the object.

2. Press **Esc** to return to the Main Menu.

3. Select **D**raw/Annotate.

4. Select **M**odify.

5. Choose **M**ove.

6. Place the target on the object you want to move
   and press **Enter**.

7. Select **C**hoose This.

8. Move the target to where you want to place the
   object and press **Enter**.

9. Press **Esc** to return to the Main Menu and save
   your modified chart.

To change the size of a selected object:

1. Display the chart with the object.

2. Press **Esc** to return to the Main Menu.

3. Select **D**raw/Annotate.

4. Select **M**odify.

5. Choose **S**ize.

6. Place the target on the object you want to size
   and press **Enter**

7. Select Choose This.

8. Use the cursor-movement keys to size the object and press Enter.

9. Press Esc to return to the Main Menu and save your modified chart.

To change the options for an object:

1. Display the chart with the object.

2. Press Esc to return to the Main Menu.

3. Select Draw/Annotate.

4. Select Modify.

5. Select Options.

6. Place the target on the object you want to change and press Enter.

7. Select Choose This.

   The Option menu is displayed.

8. Make any changes and press Enter

9. Press Esc to return to the Main Menu and save your modified chart.

To place the selected object in front or in back of another object:

1. Display the chart with the object.

2. Press Esc to return to the Main Menu.

3. Select Draw/Annotate.

4. Select Modify.

5. Select Front to move the object to the front or Back to move the object in back.

6. Place the target on the object you want to change and press Enter.

7. Select Choose This.

8. Press Esc to return to the Main Menu and save your modified chart.

Note

    See also Copying an Object and Deleting an Object.

Exporting Charts

Purpose

    Export a Harvard Graphics chart to PFS:Professional
Write or to any program that reads Encapsulated
PostScript or HPGL files. You write the chart to disk in
a format another program can read. Then you start the
second program and import the file.

Procedures

To export a chart:

1. Make the chart you want to export the Current
   Chart, and press Esc to return to the Main Menu.

2. Select Import/Export.

3. Select Export Picture.

4. Type an eight-character file name.

5. Press Tab and choose a picture quality.

   The default option is Standard. Choose High to
   create a larger file that produces a sharper print.

6. Select from PFS:Professional Write,
   Encapsulated PostScript, or HPGL formats.

7. Press F10 (Continue).

Film Recorders

Purpose

    If you have a film recorder attached to your system, you
can generate high-quality 35mm slides of your charts.

Procedures

To record the Current Chart on a film recorder:

1. From the Main Menu, select Produce Output.

2. Select Film Recorder.

3. When the Record Chart Options menu appears, type the number of copies you want to produce of the current chart.

   You may see additional options if you installed certain film recorders.

4. Press F10 (Continue).

Fonts

Purpose

Select from six fonts: Executive, Square Serif, Roman, Sans Serif, Script, and Gothic. Harvard Graphics uses the Executive font unless you choose a new default font or override the default temporarily.

Procedures

To set a new default font:

1. From the Main Menu, select Setup.

2. Select Defaults.

3. Press the Tab key, the cursor-movement keys, or the mouse to select the Font option.

4. Press the space bar to choose the font you want.

5. Press Enter.

Harvard Graphics saves the option you choose and that option becomes the new default for the program.

To override the default font temporarily:

1. Press **F8** (Options) when the Main Menu is displayed.

2. Select the font you want to use.

═ Foreign Currency Formats ═

Purpose

Shows currency values in formats other than U.S. dollars. If you want, you can reconfigure Harvard Graphics so that the British pounds currency format you choose becomes the default for all charts.

Procedures

To use foreign currency formats:

1. Make the chart you want to edit the current chart.

2. Press **F8** (Options).

3. If you are creating a pie chart, press **PgDn** and move to the Value Format field.

   If you are creating a bar/line chart, press **PgDn** and move to the Format field. Then move to the Y1 Axis option.

4. Type the foreign currency symbol.

To enter	Type
Pound	**Alt-156**
Yen	**Alt-157**
Pesetas	**Alt-158**
Guilder	**Alt-159**

5. Type a vertical line character (|).

6. Type **2** to limit the display to two decimal places.

7. Press **F2** (Draw) to preview the chart.

To make British pounds the default currency format:

1. In DOS, make the Harvard Graphics program directory the default.

   If you installed Harvard Graphics in a directory called \HG, type

   CD C:\HG

   and press Enter.

2. Type

   COPY UK.CFG HG.CFG

   and press Enter.

3. Start Harvard Graphics.

Free Form Text Charts

Purpose

Create a free form text chart when you want to control how the text aligns by positioning text manually on-screen. You can use this option, too, when you want to create more than three columns.

Procedures

To create a free form text chart:

1. At the Main Menu, press F8 (Options) if you want to change the default orientation, border, and font settings for this chart.

2. Select Create New Chart.

3. Select Text.

4. Select Free Form.

5. Type a title for the chart in the Title field.

6. Press Tab to move to the Subtitle field, and type a subtitle.

The subtitle is optional. To skip it, just press
Tab

7. Press **Tab** to move to the Footnote option.

    The footnote is optional. To skip it, just press
    Tab

8. Press **Tab** to move to the text area.

9. Type the text in any format you want.

    Press the **space bar** to enter blank spaces and
    Tab to move to the next line down.

    Note: When you indent a line, press **Enter** if you
    want the next line to be indented.

10. Press **F2** (Draw Chart) to preview the chart on
    the screen.

    If some of the lines overflow the screen, correct
    the problem by using the Size/Place command.

11. Save the chart to disk.

Notes

You can change the attributes of any text on the screen.

Add visual appeal to your pie chart with symbols,
freehand illustrations, and other enhancements using
Draw/Annotate.

After you complete your chart, perform a spell check.

See also Attributes, Draw/Annotate, Size/Place, and
Spell Check.

Getting a Chart from Disk

Purpose

Retrieves a chart so that you can edit or add
enhancements to the chart.

Procedures

To retrieve a chart you saved previously:

1. From the Main Menu, select Get/Save/Remove.

2. Select Get Chart.

3. Press the down- or up-arrow keys to select the chart file you want to retrieve.

   Press PgDn and PgUp if you have more than one screen of charts.

   If you don't see the chart you want, press F3 (Change Dir) to search other directories.

4. Press Enter.

To retrieve a chart template from a chartbook:

1. From the Main Menu, select Create new chart.

2. Select From Chartbook.

3. Press the up- and down-arrow keys to choose the template you want to retrieve.

   If you don't see the template you want, press F3 (Change Dir) to search other directories.

4. Press Enter.

Graph Charts Titles & Options

Purpose

The Bar/Line, Area, and High/Low/Close Titles & Options forms are virtually identical. All three employ a four-page menu, which contains numerous options.

Procedures

To make changes to an option form:

1. Press F8 (Options) to display the Titles & Options form.

2. Select menu items quickly by pressing **Tab** to move from item to item. Then press the **space bar** to select an option or press the option's first letter.

3. When you finish, press **F8** (Data) to return to the Chart Data menu or press **F2** (Draw) to view the chart.

To change the attributes of a text item:

1. Move the cursor to the item you want to change.

2. Press **F5** and use the cursor-movement keys to highlight the characters you want to change.

3. Press **Tab** and **Shift-Tab** to move from option to option. To select an attribute, press the **space bar.**

To change the alignment or type size of a text item:

1. Press **F7** (Size/Place).

2. Make changes to the alignment or type size.

Options

The following reference table lists options available on all three menus, as well as those options available only on the Area, Bar/Line, or High/Low/Close Titles & Options menus.

PAGE 1

Title	Type a title. Size: 8; Place: Center; Attributes: Bold, Fill.
Subtitle	Title a subtitle. Size: 6, Place: Center; Attribute: Bold, Fill.
Footnote	Type a footnote, if you want. Size: 2.5; Place: Left; Attribute: Bold, Fill.
X Axis Title	Type x-axis titles. Size: 4; Place: Center; Attribute: Bold.

Harvard Graphics enters the
x-axis data type you chose as
the x-axis title automatically.

Y1 Axis Title   Type y1 axis titles. Size: 3;
                     Place: Horizontal; Attribute:
                     Bold, Fill.

Y2 Axis Title   Type y2 axis title for paired bar
                     charts only. Size: 3; Place:
                     Horizontal; Attributes: Bold,
                     Fill.

Legend Title   Harvard Graphics automatically
                     inserts the default legend titles
                     (Series 1, Series 2, and so on).
                     Type a more descriptive title
                     here for each series you
                     entered. Attributes: Bold, Fill.

Display   Yes (default). Choose No to
                     hide the display of a series.

Y Axis   Y1 (default). Choose Y2 to
                     display a series with a y-axis
                     scale on the right side of the
                     chart (use this option in a paired
                     bar chart).

PAGE 2

Bar Width   Blank (default). Type a number
                     from 1 to 100 to control the
                     width of bars if you are creating
                     a combination chart.

3D Overlap   50 (default). Type a number
                     from 1 to 100 to control the
                     degree that areas overlap.

3D Depth	25 (default). Type a number from 1 to 100 to control the amount of depth for three-dimensional areas.
Horizontal Chart	No (default). Choose Yes to reverse the x- and y-axes, displaying the chart horizontally.
Value Labels	None (default). Choose All to place values for each item in a series at the top of all bars. Choose Select to display values for only those items for which you have chosen Yes at Y Label. Choose No to suppress the display of value labels no matter what you choose at Y Label.
Frame Style	Full (default). Choose Half to display lines only along the x- and y-axes. Choose Quarter to display a line only along the x-axis. Choose None to suppress all frame lines.
Frame Color	1 (default). Press F6 (Colors) to choose a color from the color menu.
Frame Background	0 (default). Press F6 (Colors) to choose a color from the color menu.
Legend Location	Bottom (default). Choose Top to position the legend at the top of the chart (but below the title). Choose Left to

position the legend at t left side
of the chart. Choose Right to
position the legend at the right
side of the chart. Choose None
to suppress the display of
legends (choose this option for
charts with only one data
series).

Legend
Justify

Center (default). After
choosing a legend location,
press the left- or up-arrow keys
to position the legend at the left
(if you chose a horizontal
location) or at the top (if you
chose a vertical location). Press
the down- or right-arrow key to
position the legend at the right
(if you chose a horizontal
location) or at the bottom (if
you chose a vertical location).

Legend
Placement

Out (default). Choose In
to place the legend within the
graph's frame.

Legend Frame

None (default). Choose Single
to place a single-width frame
around the legend. Choose
Double to place a double-width
frame around the legend.

PAGE 3

Data Table

None (default). Select Normal
to place a table of Y values
beneath the x-axis categories.
Select Framed to display this
table with lines around each
item.

X Axis Labels	Normal (default). Select Vertical to align the x-axis values vertically instead of horizontally. Select % to display Number values multiplied by 100. Select None to suppress the display of x-axis values.
Y1 Axis Labels	Value (default). Select $ to display the y-axis values with a dollar sign. Select % to multiply the y-axis values by 100 and display them with a percent sign. Choose None to suppress the display of y-axis values.
Y2 Axis Labels	Value (default). Select $ to display the y-axis values with a dollar sign. Select % to multiply the y-axis values by 100 and display them with a percent sign. Choose None to suppress the display of y-axis values.
X Grid Lines	None (default). Select dotted line or solid line to display grid lines within the chart frame.
Y1 Grid Lines	Broken line (default). Select dotted line or solid line to display grid lines within the chart frame.
Y2 Grid Lines	Broken line (default). Select dotted line or solid line to display grid lines within the chart frame.

| X Tick Mark Style | In (default). Select Out to display tick marks outside the x-axis. Choose Both to display tick marks that cross the x-axis. Choose None to suppress the display of tick marks. |

| Y Tick Mark Style | In (default). Select Out to display tick marks outside the y-axis. Select Both to display tick marks that cross the y-axis. Select None to suppress the display of tick marks. |

| Scale Type | Linear (default). Select Log to display data in a logarithmic scale. |

| Format | Blank (default). Type a formatting instruction to control the display of x- and y-axis values. |

| Minimum Value | 0 (y-axis) or first x-axis item (default). To override the minimum y-axis value, type the minimum number you want. |

Note: The number must be *smaller* than the smallest data point in the Chart Data form. If the number is larger than the smallest value, Harvard Graphics ignores this instruction. To tell Harvard Graphics which x-axis item you want displayed first on the chart, type the beginning x-axis item's Pt number.

Maximum Value	Automatically calculated from data in the Chart Data form (y-axis) or last x-axis item. To override the automatic maximum value y-axis value, type the maximum number to be displayed.

Note: The number must be *larger* than the largest number in the Y series data you supplied. If the number is smaller, Harvard Graphics ignores this instruction.

To tell Harvard Graphics which x-axis item to appear last on the chart, type the beginning x-axis item's Pt number (see the Chart Data form for these numbers).

Increment	Automatically supplied (y-axis); 1 (x-axis). Type a number to control the increment used to display x- or y-axis values.

PAGE 4

Cum(ulative)	No (default). Select Yes to display a running total or year-to-date sums.
Y Label	No (default). Select Yes to display y-axis values for each item in a series (above the bar or point). You must also choose Select at Value Labels. To display all y-axis values, select

	All at Value Labels instead of choosing Yes here.
Color	Press F6 (Colors) to choose colors from a menu of available options. Default varies.
Marker/Pattern	Change the number to change the mark Harvard Graphics inserts to mark data points in a line graph. Choose 0 to suppress the display of marks' entirely. Default varies.
Line Style	The default is 1 (thin, solid line). Choose 2 to display a thick, solid line. Choose 3 to display a dotted line. Choose 4 to display a dashed line.

The next sections list the options that differ for each of the three graph charts: area, bar/line, and high/low/close.

Area Chart Options

PAGE 1

Type	Area (default). Use this option to control the display of each data series independent of the others. By choosing Area for one series and Line for another, you create a combination chart. Choose Line to display the series as a zigzag line.

PAGE 2

Chart Style	Stack (default). Choose the default option to place series on top of one another, with Series

1 at the bottom. Choose Overlap to overlap the areas of two or more series. Choose 100% to stack the areas and show the contribution each series makes to the total as a percentage of the total.

Chart
Enhancement

None (default). Choose 3d to display a three-dimensional effect.

Bar/Line Chart Options

PAGE 1

Type

Bar (default). Use this option to control the display of each data series independent of the others. By choosing Bar for one series and Line for another, you create a combination chart. Choose Line to display the series as a zigzag line. Choose Trend to display the series as a trend line chart, with a best-fit trend line connecting the data points. Choose Curve to display the series as a curve line chart. Choose Pt to display the series as a data point, without connecting lines.

PAGE 2

Bar Style

Cluster (default). Choose the default option (Cluster) to group two or more series' bars together. Select Overlap to overlap the bars of two or more series.

Choose Stack to place the series' bars on top of one another, with Series 1 at the bottom. Choose 100% to stack the bars and show the contribution each series makes to the total as a percentage of the total.

Select Step to force the bars together, without any space between them. Choose Paired to create a paired bar chart with two y-axes.

Bar Enhancement	None (default). Choose 3d to display a three-dimensional effect (does not work with paired bar charts). Select Shadow to create a shadow effect on most bar charts. Choose Link to add a dotted line that connects stack and 100 percent bar charts.
Bar Fill Style	Color (default). Choose Pattern to display bars with a black and white pattern instead of color (this automatic for monochrome printers and monitors).

High/Low/Close Chart Options

PAGE 1

Type	High (Series 1), Low (Series 2), Close (Series 3), Open (Series 4). Use this option to control the display of each data series independent of the others.

By choosing Bar for one series
and Line for another, you create
a combination chart. Choose
Line to display the series as a
zigzag line. Choose Trend to
display the series as a trend line
chart, with a best-fit trend line
connecting the data points.

Choose Curve to display the
series as a curve line chart.
Choose Pt to display the series
as a data point, without
connecting lines.

PAGE 2

Bar Style

Cluster (default). Choose the
default option (Cluster) to
group two or more series
together. Choose Overlap to
overlap the bars of two or more
series. Choose Stack to place
the series on top of one another,
with Series 1 at the bottom.

High/Low
Style

Bar (default). Bar
displays the range of values
from low to high as a bar
suspended in the chart, with
tick marks for opening and
closing values.

Area displays the range of
values from low to high as an
area chart, emphasizing the
range of price variation and
implying continuity from
period to period.

Error displays the range of values from low to high as a solid line, with tick marks showing the low and high points. Additional tick marks show the opening and closing values.

Bar Fill Style
Color (default). Choose Pattern to display bars with a black and white pattern instead of color (this setting is automatic for monochrome printers and monitors).

Grid

Purpose

Shows a grid of horizontal and vertical dotted lines as you draw. Use the snap feature to force objects to align with the grid points.

Procedures

To display a grid:

1. From the Draw/Annotate menu, select Grid.

2. Select Size to change the spacing between the dotted lines.

   The default size is 4.

3. Select Yes at the Show option to see the grid on the screen.

   The default is No.

4. Select Yes at the Snap option to force objects to align with the grid.

5. Press F10 (Continue) or Enter

Note

To display x- and y-axis grids in a graph chart, see Area
Charts, Bar/Line Charts, High/Low/Close Charts as well
as Graph Charts Titles & Options.

Help

Purpose

Displays context-sensitive help screens when you press
the Help key (**F1**).

Procedures

To get on-screen help:

1. Press **F1**.

2. If you see the message, `PgDn—More help`,
   press **PgDn** to see additional screens.

3. To return to your work, press **Esc**.

High/Low/Close Charts

Purpose

Shows the high and low values of an investment at
specific intervals. You also can display the opening and
closing values. Choose from these three bar chart styles:

Bar	Shows the range of values from low to high as a bar suspended in the chart, with tick marks for opening and closing values.

Area　　　　　　　Shows the range of values from low
　　　　　　　　　to high as an area chart, emphasizing
　　　　　　　　　the range of price variation and
　　　　　　　　　implying continuity from period to
　　　　　　　　　period.

Error　　　　　　　Shows the range of values from low
　　　　　　　　　to high as a solid line, with tick
　　　　　　　　　marks showing the low and high
　　　　　　　　　points. Additional tick marks show
　　　　　　　　　the opening and closing values.

Procedures

To create a high/low/close chart:

1. At the Main Menu, press F8 (Options) to change
   the default orientation, border, and font settings.

2. Select C reate New Chart.

3. Select H igh/Low/Close.

4. When the X Data Type Menu appears, press
   Tab.

   Select D ay, W eek, M onth, Q uarter, Y ear,
   M onth/Day, M onth/Yr, or Q tr/Yr. Move to the
   Starting With field and type a starting date, time,
   or number. Type an ending date, time, or number
   at the Ending With field. You also can type an
   increment (the default is 1). When you finish,
   press F10 (Continue). If you see the message,
   Error\: X data is invalid, you
   entered the Starting With or Ending With
   information incorrectly.

5. Type a title for your chart.

6. Press Tab to go to the Subtitle field and type a
   subtitle, if desired.

7. Press Tab to go to the Footnote field and type a
   footnote, if desired.

8. Press Tab to go to the first data point and press
   Tab again to place the cursor in the High
   column. Type the high value.

9. Press **Tab** to go to the second column and type the low value.

10. Press **Tab** to go to the third column and type the closing value, if desired.

11. Press **Tab** to go to the fourth column and type the opening value, if desired.

12. Repeat Steps 8 through 11 until you type in all the data points.

13. Press **F2** to preview your chart.

14. Save the chart to disk.

Troubleshooting Tips

If you encounter problems when you press **F2** (Draw), such as the values overlapping the labels, use the many options available in the Pie Chart Titles & Options form. The following is an overview of problem-solving strategies:

- If your data includes one or two very large values and numerous small ones, you see one or two big bars while the smaller variations are illegible. You can highlight the variations among the smaller areas by selecting a logarithmic chart.

- If you have too many x-axis category names and they look squeezed together (or truncated), tab to Horizontal Chart in the High/Low/Close Chart Titles & Options form and choose **Yes**. If you do not want to display the chart horizontally, move to X Axis Labels, and select **Vertical**.

Notes

Change the attributes of the chart title, subtitle, and footnote with **F5** (Attributes).

Add visual appeal to your bar chart with symbols, freehand illustrations, and other enhancements using Draw/Annotate.

Display currency formats in foreign currencies.

Use the Values Formats field to control the display of y-axis values.

The first four data series are reserved for the High, Low, Close, and Open data. However, you can add up to four additional data series. Use these additional series to create a combination chart.

Use series calculations to copy, exchange, move, and erase data series quickly.

See also Attributes, Graph Charts Titles & Options, Draw/Annotate, Combination Chart, Currency Formats, Values Formats, and X Axis Data Types.

Histograms

Purpose

Shows a frequency distribution using stepped bars. A variation on the bar/line chart theme, you create a line chart by following the instructions for bar/line charts.

Procedures

To create a histogram:

1. Follow the instructions for bar/line charts to enter initial data.

   When you see the X Data Type Menu, select Name and type the frequency distribution in the X Axis column. Then add the data series (up to a maximum of eight).

2. Press F8 (Options).

3. Press PgDn and tab to the Bar Style field.

4. Select Step.

5. Press F2 to preview your chart.

6. Save the chart to disk.

Note

See also Bar/Line Charts.

Importing ASCII Data

Purpose

Imports ASCII text to a text chart. If the ASCII file
contains data that are grouped into tabular columns
separated by at least three spaces, you can import ASCII
data to a graph chart. The file must have exactly the
right format. The first line or column must contain the X
axis labels, while the second line or column must
contain the first Y data series, and so on.

Procedures

To import ASCII data:

1. From the Main Menu, select Create New Chart.

   If you select a bar/line, area, or high/low/close
   chart, select an X Axis Data Type that matches
   the x-axis data in your worksheet.

2. Press Esc to return to the Main Menu.

3. Select Import/Export.

4. Select Import ASCII Data.

5. When you see the Select File form, press the
   down- or up-arrow key to highlight the name of
   the Lotus worksheet that contains the graph you
   want to import.

   If you do not see the file you want, press F3
   (Change dir).

6. Press F10 (Continue).

   When you see the Import ASCII Data form, you
   see the first thirteen lines of the file.

   Use the cursor-movement keys to move around
   in the file, as if you were using a text editor.

7. Specify the text to read.

At the Read Data By field, select the Line option
to read every line of the chart. To tell Harvard
Graphics to read only some lines, specify the
beginning line at the Read From Line field and
the ending line at the To Line field. You also can
select the text to read by specifying a specific
column. Choose Column at the Read Data By
field, and specify the beginning and ending
column. If the data are in tabular form, select
Yes at the Tabular Data Format field.

8. Press F10 to import the data.

Importing Lotus 1-2-3 Data

Purpose

Imports data directly from a Lotus 1-2-3 worksheet to a
Harvard Graphics chart data form. From this form, you
can generate a variety of charts and graphs. Before you
import Lotus data, make a note of the cell ranges that
contain the X axis category names and the Y axis data
series. You must specify this information to import the
Lotus data.

Harvard Graphics can read Lotus 1-2-3 graphs directly.
You can import a Lotus graph easier than you can
import a Lotus spreadsheet. When you import a graph,
you need not specify the cell ranges of the x- and y-axis
data. You specified this information when you created
the Lotus Graph, and Harvard Graphics reads this
information directly.

To import a graph, you import from the worksheet file,
not the .PIC file you create when you save a Lotus graph
to disk.

Procedures

To import Lotus data:

1. From the Main Menu, select Create New Chart.

If you select a bar/line, area, or high/low/close chart, choose an X Axis Data Type that matches the x-axis data in your Lotus worksheet.

2. Press Esc to return to the Main Menu.

3. Select Import/Export.

4. Select Import Lotus Data.

5. When you see the Select Worksheet form, press the up- or down-arrow keys to highlight the name of the Lotus worksheet that contains the graph you want to import.

   If you do not see the graph you want, press F3 (Change dir).

6. Type cell references and cell address ranges for titles, x-axis categories, and y-data series.

   You can use range names you created with Lotus.

7. Press F10 (Continue).

   You see the Import Lotus Data screen.

8. If you want, change the file name at the Graph Name field. Select No at the Import Data Only field.

9. Press F10.

To import a Lotus graph:

1. From the Main Menu, select Import/Export.

2. Select Import Lotus Graph.

3. When you see the Select Worksheet form, press the up- and down-arrow keys to highlight the name of the Lotus worksheet that contains the graph you want to import.

   If you do not see the graph you want, press F3 (Change dir).

4. Press **F10** (Continue).

   You see the Import Lotus Graph screen.

5. If you want, change the file name at the Graph Name field. Select **N**o at the Import Data Only field.

6. Press **F10**

Note

If you see the message `no charts were found`, make sure that you created a graph in the Lotus worksheet you named.

Insert Mode

Purpose

The characters you type push existing characters right. By default, Harvard Graphics operates in an overtype text entry mode. When you place the cursor on existing text and type new characters, the new characters rub out existing text.

Harvard Graphics does not save your choice. The next time you start the program, the overtype mode is in effect.

Procedure

To turn on or off Insert mode, press **Ins**

Note

When the insert mode is on, the cursor resembles a rectangle rather than an underline character.

Installing Harvard Graphics

Floppy Disk System

Purpose

To use Harvard Graphics on a system with two 3 1/2-inch disk drives, you begin by making backup copies of the Program and Utilities disks. Then you prepare a working data disk that contains certain files Harvard Graphics requires.

Procedures

To make working copies of the Harvard Graphics disks:

1. Prepare three blank, formatted disks.

   Two of these disks are used in this tutorial. The third is used in the next tutorial.

2. Insert the Harvard Graphics Program disk in drive A.

3. Put a blank, formatted disk in drive B.

4. Type **COPY A:*.* B:** and press **Enter**.

5. Remove the disk from drive B. Label the disk *Harvard Graphics Program Disk\: Backup Copy.*

6. Place the Utilities disk in drive A.

7. Place the second blank, unformatted disk in drive B.

8. Type **MD B:\VDI** and press **Enter**.

9. Type **COPY A:\VDI B:\VDI** and press **Enter**.

10. Type **COPY A:*.* B:** and press **Enter**.

11. Remove the disk from drive B. Label the disk *Harvard Graphics Utilities Disk: Backup Copy.*

To prepare a working data disk:

1. Insert the Symbols disk in drive A.

2. Place the third blank, unformatted disk in drive B.

3. Type **COPY A:*.FNT B:** and press **Enter**.

4. Type **COPY A:*.PAL B:** and press **Enter**.

5. Remove the disk from drive B. Label the disk *Working Chart Disk*.

Notes

You may find it useful to make several backup copies of your Working Chart disk. Because so much room is occupied by Harvard Graphics files, the working chart disk fills up quickly and you soon will find yourself requiring another. Use the DOS DISKCOPY command to make additional copies of this disk.

Use the backup copies of the Program and Utilities disks, not the originals, for everyday work.

See also Film Recorders, Plotters, and Printers for information on installing these devices.

Installing Harvard Graphics

Hard Disk System

Purpose

You copy the program and all the Harvard Graphics files to a backup disk or to your hard disk. Unless your hardware setup matches the choices in the program's default settings, however, you must choose new defaults.

You begin by using the Install program on the Utilities Disk. Then you create a data directory to store your Harvard Graphics charts. Finally, you create a PATH statement to tell DOS where to find the Harvard Graphics program.

The installation process takes about 15 minutes to complete, and Harvard Graphics occupies approximately 1.7 megabytes of space on your hard disk. You can reduce this space amount somewhat by erasing printer and plotter files you are not using.

Procedures

To use the Install program:

1. Insert the Utilities disk in drive A.

2. Type A:\ and press Enter to obtain the A> prompt.

3. Type INSTALL and press Enter

4. When you see the prompt, `Type the drive letter and directory of the DESTINATION disk`, type C:\HG and press Enter

5. When you see the message, `Could not find the subdirectory`, press Y and press Enter to create the subdirectory.

   Harvard Graphics creates a new subdirectory on your hard disk and begins copying files.

6. Follow the instructions on the screen.

   You are asked to insert the Harvard Graphics disks, one after the other.

To create a data directory:

1. With the C> prompt displayed on the screen, type CD\ to make sure that the root directory is selected.

2. Type CD \HG to select the directory you created when you installed Harvard Graphics.

3. Type MD \HGDATA and press Enter

   You must tell Harvard Graphics that you want the program to save your graphics to the Data directory you created.

To tell Harvard Graphics where to store your charts:

1. Start Harvard Graphics.

2. From the Main Menu, select Setup.

3. Select Defaults.

4. Type C:\HG\HGDATA and press Enter.

5. Press F10 to return to the Main Menu.

To tell DOS where to find the Harvard Graphics program:

Add the statement PATH = C:\HG to your AUTOEXEC.BAT file.

If your system does not currently have an AUTOEXEC.BAT file, create and add the statement.

To create the file AUTOEXEC.BAT and add the path statement:

1. In DOS, type C:\ to make sure that the root directory is selected.

2. Type COPY CON AUTOEXEC.BAT and press Enter.

3. Type PATH = C:\HG.

4. Press Ctrl-Z.

5. Press Enter.

Note

See Film Recorders, Plotters, and Printers for information on installing these devices.

Keywords—Row Calculation

This section contains a reference guide to the keywords you can use with row calculation.

@AVG   ***Example:*** @AVG(#1,#2,#3)

Calculates the average row values. In the example, Harvard Graphics calculates the average of Series 1, 2, and 3 across the row, and places the average in a new series

@MAX   ***Example:*** @MAX(#1,#2,#3)

Finds the maximum value in row values. In this example, Harvard Graphics finds the largest value in the row that crosses Series 1, 2, and 3, and places this value in a new series.

@MIN   ***Example:*** @MIN(#1,#2,#3)

Finds the minimum value in row values. In this example, Harvard Graphics finds the largest value in the row that crosses Series 1, 2, and 3, and places this value in a new series.

@SUM   ***Example:*** @SUM(#1,#2,#3)

Sums the row values. In this example Harvard Graphics adds the values in the row that crosses Series 1, 2, and 3 and places the sum in a new series.

Keywords—Series Calculation

This section contains a reference guide to the keywords you can use with series calculation.

@CLR   ***Example:*** @CLR

Erases the values in the current series. Use this keyword to clear all the values in a series instead of deleting them one by one. After you use this keyword, Harvard Graphics erases it from the series.

@COPY   *Example:* @COPY(#1)

Copies the values from another series. In this example, Harvard Graphics copies the values from Series 1 to the current series. After you use this keyword, Harvard Graphics erases it from the series.

@CUM   *Example:* @CUM(#1)

Calculates the cumulative total of values in a series by adding each data point to the total of all previous data points in the series. In this example, Harvard Graphics calculates the cumulative values of Series 1 and places the running total in the current series.

@DIFF   *Example:* @DIFF(#1)

Calculates the net change (not percentage change) between a data point and the previous data point, and repeats this calculation for the whole series. In this example, Harvard Graphics calculates the difference between successive data points for all the values of Series 1 (except the first) and places the differences in the current series.

@DUP   *Example:* @DUP(#1)

Copies the values in a series to the current series, and updates the values when you alter or recalculate them. In this example, Harvard Graphics copies the values in Series 1 to the current series. The program updates the current series when you make changes in Series 1.

Note: Updates occur only when you press **F10** when the Calculate menu is displayed or use the @RECALC instruction. Use this series to display a data series in two different ways (for example, in a bar graph and in a trend line).

@EXCH   *Example:* @EXCH(#1)

Exchanges the values in a series (and the series' legend) with the current series. In the example, Harvard Graphics swaps the values in the current series with the values in Series 1.

Use this instruction to change the order in which series appear in the Chart Data form. After you use this keyword, Harvard Graphics erases it from the series.

@MAVG   *Example:* @MAVG(#1)

Calculates the moving average of values in a series. You can specify the number of points before and after to use in calculating the moving average. If you do not specify the points before and after, Harvard Graphics uses one point before and one point after. In the example, the program calculates the moving average for Series 1 using one point before and after.

@MOVE   *Example:* @MOVE(#1)

Moves a data series to the current series. In this example, Harvard Graphics moves Series 1 to the current series. *Note:* Harvard Graphics erases values in the current series. You can use this instruction to rearrange data series. However, if the current series contains data you want to save, use the @EXCH instruction. After you use this keyword, Harvard Graphics erases it from the series.

@PCT   *Example:* @PCT(#1)

Calculates the percent contribution of each value in a series to the total of all the values in the series. In this example, Harvard Graphics calculates the percent contribution of each value in Series 1 and places the results in the current series.

@REDUC   *Example:* @REDUC

Performs automatic data reduction and reordering on all series in the Chart Data form. For information, see Data Reduction. This instruction may prove useful after you

import data in which X labels are duplicated or missing.
After you use this keyword, Harvard Graphics erases it
from the series.

***

@RECALC   *Example:* @RECALC

Recalculates the series if you made changes to the
original data. For instance, suppose that Series 2
contains a moving average of the data in Series 1, but
you changed one of the Series 1 data points. Series 2
will not contain the correct data until you use the
@RECALC instruction. After you use this keyword,
Harvard Graphics erases it from the series.

***

@REXP   *Example:* @REXP(#1)

Calculates the exponential regression curve for a series.
In this example, Harvard Graphics calculates the
exponential regression curve of Series 1 and places the
curve's data points in the current series. *Caution:* Do
not select the Trend line type for the series you calculate
with @REXP. The Trend line employs a linear
regression formula and produces erroneous results in
combination with @REXP.

***

@RLIN   *Example:* @RLIN (#1)

Calculates the linear regression curve for a series. In this
example, Harvard Graphics calculates the exponential
regression curve of Series 1 and places the curve's data
points in the current series.

Calculates the logarithmic regression curve for a series.
In this example, Harvard Graphics calculates the
logarithmic regression curve of Series 1 and places the
curve's data points in the current series.

***

@RPWR   *Example:* @RPWR (#1)

Calculates the power regression curve for a series. In
this example, Harvard Graphics calculates the power
regression curve of Series 1 and places the curve's data
points in the current series.

Line Charts

Purpose

A variation on the Bar/Line Chart theme. You create a line chart by following the instructions for bar/line charts. Choose from the following line chart formats:

Zigzag	Harvard Graphics connects the data points with straight lines, resulting in a zigzagging line.
Trend	Harvard Graphics automatically calculates a straight line of best fit.
Curve	Harvard Graphics automatically calculates a curved line of best fit.

Procedures

To create a line chart:

1. Follow the instructions for bar/line charts to enter initial data.

2. Press F8 (Options).

3. On page 1 of the Bar/Line Chart Titles & Options form, tab to the table at the bottom of the screen that contains the series legend titles.

4. Place the cursor on the Series 1 field and press Tab.

5. Select Line, Trend, or Curve.

6. Repeat Steps 4 and 5 for additional data series.

7. Press PgDn to see Page 4 of the Bar/Line Chart Titles & Options form.

8. Press Tab to move to the table at the bottom of the screen that contains the series legend titles.

9. Place the cursor on the first data series you defined.

10. Press Tab to move to the Marker/Pattern field and select a different marker pattern, if you want.

You can choose from the following 13 marker patterns: 0—none, 1—dot, 2—plus, 3—asterisk, 4—square, 5—x, 6—diamond, 7—up triangle, 8—partially boxed X, 9—circle, 10—down triangle, 11—star, 12—boxed X, 13—outline plus.

11. Press Tab to move to the Line Style field and choose a different line style.

    You can choose from the following four line styles: 1—thin, 2—thick, 3—dotted, and 4—dashed.

12. Repeat Steps 9 through 11 for additional data series.

13. Press F2 to preview your chart.

14. Save the chart to disk.

Note

See also Bar/Line Charts and Trend Line Charts.

Linked Pie/Column Charts

Purpose

Shows the parts of a whole. If you want to focus attention on one of the slices and show how the slice is further broken down into components, create a linked pie/column chart. Although you can link two pies or two columns, the most effective approach is to display a pie on the left and a column on the right.

Procedures

To create and link two pie/column charts:

1. Create the first pie or column chart following the instructions for pie charts or column charts.

    The labels and values you type should be those of the whole.

2. Type **Y** in the Cut Slice column for the slice you want to link.

3. Press **PgDn** to see Page 2 of the Pie Chart Data form.

   You see the message `Pie Chart 2 Data, Page 2 of 2` at the top of the screen. Under the Values option, you see Series 2.

   The labels and values you type on this form should represent a breakdown of the slice you pulled out of Pie 1.

4. Type the labels and values of the second pie or column chart.

5. Press **F8** (Options) to see the Pie Chart Titles & Options form.

6. Tab to the Pie 1 Title field and type a title for the first pie. Then tab to the Pie 2 Title field and type a title for the second one.

7. Tab to the Link Pies option and choose **Yes**.

8. Press **PgDn** to see Page 2 of the Pie Chart Titles & Options form.

9. Tab to the Chart Style field under Pie 2 and select **Column**.

10. Press **F2** to preview your chart.

11. Save the chart to disk.

Troubleshooting Tips

In the Pie Chart Titles & Options form, you can perform these problem solving steps:

- If the display looks cluttered with too many values, tab to the Show Value field in the Pie Chart Titles & Options form and, for Pie 2, choose **No** to suppress the display of values.

- Tab to the Place Value field and the Place Percent field in the Pie Chart Titles & Options form and, for Pie 2, choose Adjacent to display the values next to the labels so that they don't overlap.

See also Pie Charts, Pie Chart Titles & Options Form, and Column Charts.

Logarithmic Charts

Purpose

Use when the data you want to present are highly variable. A logarithmic scale replaces the linear y-axis scaling (such as 10, 20, 30, and so on) with one in which the increments represent orders of magnitude (10, 100, 1000, 10000, 100000, and so on). Such a scale accommodates the larger values without compressing the smaller values.

An area chart, bar/line chart, or high/low/close chart may fail to show the smaller data points legibly. For instance, suppose that you create a bar chart where most of the bars reach only to 40 or 50, but one reaches to 6,000. To accommodate the largest bar, Harvard Graphics uses a linear scale that compresses the smallest bars so much that you cannot see the differences among them.

You can scale both the x- and the y-axes logarithmically. If you scale both axes logarithmically, the chart is known as a *log-log chart*. For most purposes, you use a log scale for the y-scale only.

Procedures

To scale the y-axis logarithmically:

1. Follow the instructions for bar/line charts to enter initial data.

When you see the X Data Type Menu, choose
Name and type the frequency distribution in the
X Axis column. Then add the data series (up to a
maximum of eight).

2. Press F8 (Options).

3. Press PgDn until you see Page 3.

4. Press Tab to go to the Scale Type field and tab
   over to Y1 Axis.

5. Select Log.

6. Press F2 to preview your chart.

═ **Multiple Charts** ══════════════════════════

Purpose

Creates a single chart that contains up to six different
charts. Use Draw/Annotate to add annotations, boxes,
and other effects to your multiple chart.

Procedures

To create a multiple chart:

1. From the Main Menu, select Create New Chart.

2. Select Multiple Charts.

3. Select Custom, Two, Three, or Four.

   Choose Custom if you want to design your own
   layout. Select the other options if you want to
   use Harvard Graphics' built-in layout options for
   two, three, or four chart layouts.

   You see the Edit Multiple Chart form. The top
   half lists the charts in the current directory, and
   the bottom half lists the charts to be inserted in
   your multiple chart.

4. In the top half of the form, use the up- or down-arrow keys to select a chart to include in your multiple chart and press **Enter**.

   Press **Tab** to move from the bottom half to the top half of the chart, if necessary.

5. Repeat Step 4 until all the charts you want to include in your multiple chart are chosen.

6. If you chose a predefined layout, just press **F10** (Continue).

7. If you chose the Custom option, Press **F7** (Size/Place) to see the custom chart layout screen.

8. Highlight the chart you want to place from the list.

9. Move the target to the place you want the upper left corner of the chart to appear, and press **Enter**. Then use the cursor-movement keys to expand the box to the lower right corner. Press **Enter** again to complete the placement.

10. Repeat Steps 8 and 9 until you finish placing charts where you want them. Then Press **F10** (Continue).

Note

See also Draw/Annotate.

Normalized (100%) Bar Charts

Purpose

Shows the percent contribution each series makes to a whole. However, you can create only two normalized columns using the column chart format. A variation on the bar/line chart theme, normalized (100%) bar charts permit you to show more than two bars that display percent contributions.

Procedures

To create a normalized (100%) bar chart:

1. Follow the instructions for bar/line charts to enter initial data.

2. Press **F8** (Options).

3. Press **PgDn** to see Page 2 of the Bar/Line Chart Titles & Options form.

4. Select 100% at the Bar Style field.

5. Press **F2** to preview your chart.

6. Save the chart to disk.

Numbered List Text Chart

Purpose

A variation on the bulleted list text chart, a numbered list chart shows items in numerical order. Harvard Graphics numbers the items automatically.

Procedures

To create a numbered list text chart:

1. At the Main Menu, press **F8** (Options) to change the default orientation, border, and font settings for this chart.

2. Select Create New Chart.

3. Select Text.

4. Select Bullet List.

5. At the Title field, type a title for the chart.

6. Press **Tab** to move to the Subtitle field and type a subtitle.

The subtitle is optional. To skip it, just press **Tab**.

7. Press **Tab** to move to the Footnote field.

   The footnote is also optional. To skip it, just press **Tab**.

8. Press **Tab** to move to the bulleted list area.

9. Press **F7** to select the Size/Place command.

10. Use the cursor-movement keys to select the Bullet Shape area.

11. Press the **space bar** to select the automatic number character (#).

12. Press **F10** (Continue).

13. Type the first item in the list.

14. Press **Enter** twice.

15. Type the next item in the list.

16. Repeat Steps 14 and 15 to complete the chart.

17. Press **F2** (Draw Chart) to preview the chart.

    If some of the lines overflow the screen, correct the problem by using the Size/Place command.

18. Save the chart to disk.

Notes

You can change the attributes of any text on-screen.

Add visual appeal to your pie chart with symbols, freehand illustrations, and other enhancements using Draw/Annotate.

After you complete your chart, perform a spell check.

See also Attributes, Draw/Annotate, Spell Check, and Size/Place.

Organization Charts

Purpose

Useful for describing the structure of authority and
responsibility in an organization—the chain of
command. Harvard Graphics organization charts can
display up to eight levels of hierarchy and 80 members
or departments. After you create the chart, you can
format the title, subtitle, and footnote, and edit the list of
subordinates.

Procedures

To create an organization chart:

1. At the Main Menu, press **F8** (Options) to change
   the default orientation, border, and font settings
   for this chart.

2. Select Create New Chart.

3. Select Organization.

4. At the Title field, type a title for the chart.

5. Press **Tab** to move to the Subtitle field and type
   a subtitle.

   The subtitle is optional. To skip it, just press
   Tab.

6. Press **Tab** to move to the Footnote option.

   The footnote is also optional. To skip it, just
   press **Tab**.

7. Press **Tab** to move to the Name field, and type
   the name and title of the top-ranking official of
   the organization.

   Harvard Graphics is preset to show the title as
   well as the name.

8. Press **Tab** to move to the Subordinates column
   and type the names of all second-ranking persons
   who report directly to the top-ranking official.

9. To add subordinates to a second-ranking official, place the cursor on the official's name in the Subordinates column. Then press **Ctrl-PgDn**.

    The second ranking official's name is now listed in the Manager's column. Press **Tab** to move to the Subordinates field and type the names of the third-ranking officials.

    You can add up to eight levels of subordinates, each with subordinates. To move back up the hierarchy, press **Ctrl-PgUp**. To move to the screens of other subordinates at the same level, press **PgUp** and **PgDn.**

10. Press **F2** (Draw Chart) to preview the chart.

11. Save the chart to disk.

To edit an organization chart:

Use these special procedures for editing the subordinate list:

*   To change the order in which subordinates are listed, place the cursor on the subordinate's name in the Subordinates box and press **Ctrl-up arrow** or **Ctrl-down arrow**.

*   To add a subordinate's name within the list, place the cursor where you want the subordinate's name to appear, and press **Ctrl-Ins**.

*   To delete a subordinate's name, place the cursor on the name and press **Ctrl-Del**.

Keys

Use these keystrokes when you create an organization chart:

PgDn	Displays the Organization Chart form for the next subordinate at the same level.

PgUp	Displays the Organization Chart form for the previous subordinate at the same level.
Ctrl-PgDn	Displays the Organization Chart form for the subordinate on whose name the cursor is positioned.
Ctrl-PgUp	Displays the next higher level manager.
Ctrl-Ins	Adds a blank line in the subordinate list.
Ctrl-Del	Deletes a subordinate's name from the list.
Ctrl-↑	In the subordinate list, moves a subordinate's name up the list.
Ctrl-↓	In the subordinate list, moves a subordinate's name down the list.

Options

Use the following Organization options:

Start Chart At	Top (default). Select Current manager to display the currently-displayed manager at the top level.
Levels to Show	All (default). Select a number from 1 to 7 to control the number of levels displayed (counting from top).
Show Titles	Yes (default). Select No to hide titles.

Show Comments	No (the default). Select Yes to display comments.
Abbreviations	No (default). Select Yes to display abbreviations.
Shadow	No (default). Select Yes to display each box with a shadow effect.
Names	Light (default). Select Italic or Bold to change the emphasis.
Names Color	Press F6 (Colors) to select from a list of available colors.
Names Split	Yes (default). Select No to keep both parts of a name on the same line.
Titles	Italic (default). Select Light or Bold to change the emphasis.
Titles Color	Press F6 (Colors) to select from a list of available colors.
Titles Split	No (default). Select Yes to split a two-word title over two lines.
Comments	Light (default). Select Italic or Bold to change emphasis.
Comments Color	Press F6 (Colors) to select from a list of available colors.
Comments Split	No (default). Select Yes to split a two-word comment over two lines.
Last Level Show Titles	No (default). Select Yes to display titles of last-level subordinates.

| Last Level
Show Comments | No (default). Select Yes to display comments about last-level subordinates. |
| Last Level
Arrangement | Vertical (default). Select Horizontal to display last-level names in horizontally aligned boxes like the rest of the chart. |

Notes

You can add drawings, symbols, and text to your chart using Draw/Annotate.

Use spell check after creating your chart.

To control the attributes, size, and placement of the chart title, subtitle, and footnote, use the F5 (Attributes) and F7 (Size/Place) keys.

By default, Harvard Graphics displays all levels of an organization chart. Titles are shown in italics, but comments and abbreviations are hidden. Names are split on two lines. The last level is shown in a vertical list format instead of horizontal boxes.

See also Attributes, Draw/Annotate, and Size/Place.

Orientation

Purpose

Harvard Graphics is preset to print your charts and graphs in Landscape orientation (horizontally on the page). The Landscape orientation is best for most purposes, but if you want, you can change the default setting. You also can override the default setting temporarily so that only the current chart is affected.

Procedures

To set a new default orientation:

1. From the Main Menu, select Setup.

2. Select Defaults.

3. Use the Tab key, the cursor-movement keys, or the mouse to move to the Orientation field.

4. Press the space bar to select Landscape (horizontal) or Portrait (vertical).

5. Press Enter.

Harvard Graphics saves the option you choose and it becomes the new default for the program.

To override the default orientation temporarily:

1. From the Main Menu, press F8 (Options).

2. Select the orientation you want.

Paired Bar Charts

Purpose

A variation on bar/line charts, paired bar charts are useful for comparing two data series that share the same x-axis categories. When you create a paired bar chart, Harvard Graphics displays the two data series horizontally along a common vertical axis at the center of the chart.

Procedures

To create a paired bar chart:

1. Follow the instructions for bar/line charts to create a bar chart with two data series.

2. Press F8 (Options).

3. Press Tab to go to the Series 2 field in the list at the bottom of Page 1.

4. Press Tab to go to the Y Axis column and select the Y2 option.

5. Press PgDn.

6. At the Bar Style field, choose Paired.

7. Press **F2** (Draw) to preview your paired bar
    chart.

Pie Charts

Purpose

Use a single pie chart to show the parts of a whole, such
as the contributions of sales regions to the total sales
picture.

Procedures

To create a pie chart:

1. At the Main Menu, press **F8** (Options) to change
    the default orientation, border, and font settings
    for this chart.

2. Select Create New Chart.

3. Select Pie.

4. Type a title for your chart and press **Tab**.

5. If you want a subtitle, type a name and press
    Tab.

6. If you want a footnote, type one and press **Tab**.

7. Under the Label field, type the label you want to
    appear on the chart next to a pie slice. You can
    type a name up to 20 characters in length.

    To split the label so that it is displayed on two
    lines, type a vertical character (|) where you want
    the split to occur.

8. Press **Enter** to move to the next slice down in
    the Label column, and type the second label.
    Continue pressing **Enter** and typing labels until
    you type all the labels.

9. Press **Tab** to go to the Slice 1 Value column and type a value.

    Do not type dollar signs or commas.

10. Press **Enter** to move to the next slice down in the Value column, and type the second label. Continue pressing **Enter** and typing values until you have typed all the values.

11. Press **F2** to preview your chart.

12. Save the chart to disk.

___

Notes

Change the attributes of the chart title, subtitle, and footnote using **F5** (Attributes).

Add visual appeal to your pie chart with symbols, freehand illustrations, and other enhancements using Draw/Annotate

The Pie Chart Titles & Options form lists many options for displaying your pie chart. The following is a quick overview of commonly used options:

- To show the slices in order of magnitude (rather than the order you typed them), tab to the Sort Slices field and select **Yes**.

- To show values in currency, tab to the Currency field, and select **Yes**. Then tab to the Value Format field and type **,2** (a comma followed by the number 2).

- To show percentages next to each value, tab to the Show Percent field and select **Yes**.

- To show the pie with a three-dimensional effect, tab to the 3D Effect field and choose **Yes**.

- A *cut slice* is a pie chart slice that has been drawn away from the pie for emphasis. To display a cut slice, place the cursor on the slice's label name in the Chart Data form. Then tab to the Cut Slice field and choose **Yes**.

Keys

Use the following keys when you create a pie chart:

PgDn	Moves to the next page of Pie Chart Titles & Options form.
PgUp	Moves to the previous page of Pie Chart Titles & Options form.
Ctrl-Ins	In the Chart Data form, inserts a blank line in slice list to make room for a new slice label.
Ctrl-Del	In the Chart Data form, deletes a line in the slice list.
Ctrl-↑	In the Chart Data form, moves the current slice up in the list.
Ctrl-↓	In the Chart Data form, moves the current slice down in the list.

Troubleshooting Tips

If you encounter problems when you press **F2** (Draw), such as titles overlapping one another, repair the errors with the many options available in the Pie Chart Titles and Options menu. The following is a quick overview of problem solving strategies:

- If the labels are unattractively situated, rotate the pie by typing a rotation factor next to the Starting Angle field in the Pie Chart Titles & Options form.

- If the pie or the labels interfere with the title, type a smaller pie size next to the Pie Size field in the Pie Chart Titles & Options form.

- If the labels are too large or some labels are truncated because they do not fit on-screen, reduce the type size by typing a smaller number next to the Label Size field in the Pie Chart Titles & Options form.

- If you are displaying or printing your pie chart in monochrome, Harvard Graphics uses patterns instead of color. If the pattern set up is moiré vibrations, try changing the patterns by typing different pattern numbers in the Pattern column of the Chart Data form.

Note

See also Attributes, Draw/Annotate, Pie Chart Titles and Options Menu, Column Charts, Linked Pie/Column Charts, and Two Pie Charts.

Pie Chart Titles & Options

Purpose

A two-page menu, which contains numerous options for pie charts. Use this form to control the appearance of virtually every component on a bar or line chart. In addition, use this form to create variations on the pie chart theme, such as column charts, linked pie/column charts, and two pie charts.

Procedures

To make changes to the chart options:

1. Press F8 (Options) to display the Pie Chart Titles & Options form.

2. Choose menu items quickly by pressing Tab to move from item to item. Then press the space bar to choose an option or press the option's first letter.

3. When you finish, press F8 (Data) to return to the Chart Data menu or press F2 (Draw) to view the chart.

To change the attributes of a text item:

1. Move the cursor to the item you want to change.

2. Press F5 and use the cursor-movement keys to highlight the characters you want to change.

3. Press **Tab** and **Shift-Tab** to move from option to
   option. To select an attribute, press the **space
   bar**.

To change the alignment or type size of a text item:

1. Press **F7** (Size/Place).

2. Make changes to the alignment or type size.

PAGE 1

Title
: Type a title.

  Size, 8; Place: Center;
  Attribute: Bold, Fill. Type a
  chart title.

Subtitle
: Type a chart subtitle (optional).
  Size: 6; Place: Center;
  Attribute: Bold, Fill.

Footnote
: Type a footnote (optional).
  Size: 2.5; Place: Left; Attribute:
  Bold, Fill.

Pie 1 Title
: Type a Pie 1 title (optional).
  Size: 5; Place: Left; Attribute:
  Fill.

Pie 2 Title
: Type a Pie 2 title (optional).
  Size: 5; Place: Left; Attribute:
  Fill.

3D Effect
: No (default). Choose Yes to
  display the pie or column with a
  3-D effect.

Link Pies
: Choose Yes to display Pie or
  Column 2 as a breakdown of
  one of the slices in Pie or
  Column 1. Choose No (default)
  to display two pies or columns
  in which the values are
  independent of each other.

Proportional
Pies

No (default). Choose Yes
to display two pies so that pie
with the larger total value is
displayed proportionally larger
than the other pie.

Fill Style

Choose Color (default) to
display the pie or column in the
colors set on the Chart Data
form. Choose Pattern to display
the pie or column with black
and white patterns. Choose
Both to display with colors and
patterns

PAGE 2

Chart Style

Pie (default). Choose Column
to display the data as a
normalized (100%) column
chart. Choose None under Pie 2
to limit the display to a single
Pie 1 chart.

Sort Slices

Choose Yes to sort the slices
and display them in order of
size, ranging from largest to
smallest. Choose No (default)
to display the slices in the order
you listed them in the Chart
Data menu.

Starting Angle

0 (default). Type a number
from 0 to 360 to rotate the pie.
Type 90 to rotate the pie.

Pie Size

50 (default). To change the size
of the pie, type a number from
0 to 100. Press F2 (Draw) to
see the effect of the change.

Show Label   Yes (default). Choose No to
                    suppress the display of labels.

Label Size   3 (default). Type 1 or 2 to
                    reduce the size of the labels;
                    type a larger number to enlarge
                    them.

Show Value   Yes (default). Choose No to
                    hide the display of values and
                    percentages.

Place Value   Below (default). Choose
                    Adjacent to display the values
                    next to the label. Choose Inside
                    to display the values inside the
                    slice.

Value Format   Blank (default).

Currency   No (default). Choose Yes to
                    display all values preceded by
                    the default currency symbol ($
                    for North American systems).

Show Percent   No (default). Choose Yes to
                    display a percentage with to
                    each value. The percentage is
                    automatically calculated by
                    totalling the values of the pie.

Place Percent   Below. (default). Choose
                    Adjacent to display the
                    percentage next to the label.
                    Choose Inside to display the
                    percentage inside the slice.

Percent Format   Blank, displays percentages as
                  integers, as in 44% (default).
                  Type a whole number from 1
                  through 9 to display fractions of
                  a percent (as in 44.18%). Type
                  1 to display percentages in
                  scientific notation.

Plotters

Purpose

Harvard Graphics works with a wide variety of plotters.
You can print charts that contain up to eight colors plus
black, even if your plotter doesn't have that many pen
holders.

Procedures

To specify the plotter you are using:

1. From the Main Menu, select Setup.

2. Select Plotter.

3. Use the cursor-movement keys or the mouse to
   select the plotter you are using.

4. When you see the Parallel/Serial overlay
   window, highlight the port to which your printer
   is connected (LPT1, LPT2, COM1, COM2, or
   COM3).

   If you selected a serial port (one of the COM
   options), change the default baud rate, parity,
   data bits, and stop bits settings if necessary.
   Consult your plotter manual to determine the
   proper settings.

5. Press **Enter**.

Harvard Graphics saves the option you choose and the setting becomes the new default for the program.

To tell Harvard Graphics to pause as you manually change pen colors:

Select the Yes option at the Pause for Pen field in the Plot Chart Options menu. You see this option when you print your chart.

Note

See also Printing with a Plotter.

Point Charts

Purpose

A variation on bar/line charts, point charts show data as points that are not connected by lines. Point charts, which are also called *scatter diagrams,* are widely used in scientific applications. When several data series are shown, clusters of points—representing data correlations—become obvious.

Procedures

To create a point chart:

1. Follow the instructions for bar/line charts to enter the data.

2. Press **F8** (Options).

3. Press **Tab** to move to the Type column at the bottom of the screen and press the down-arrow key to select the first data series' type.

4. Select **Pt.**

5. Repeat Steps 3 and 4 for all data series.

6. Press **F2** (Draw) to preview your chart.

Polygons

Purpose

Use Draw/Annotate to add polygons to your chart.

Procedures

To draw a polygon:

1. Display your chart and then press Esc until you see the Main Menu.

2. Select Draw/Annotate.

3. Select Add.

4. Select Polygon.

5. Press F8 (Options) to select polygon options.

6. Press F8 (Draw) to draw the circle or ellipse.

7. Move the target to a point on the polygon and press Enter.

8. Use the cursor-movement keys to move the target.

9. Move the target to draw one side of the polygon and press Enter.

10. Repeat Step 9 until you complete the polygon.

    You can delete the last segment you entered by pressing the Backspace key.

11. Press Enter to complete the polygon.

12. Press Esc to return to the Add menu.

Options

You can use these Polygon Options:

Outline Draw   Yes (default). Draw an outline around the polygon. Choose No if you filled the center of the polygon with a distinctive color.

Outline Color	Default color depends on your hardware. Press F6 (Choices) to choose colors from a menu.
Center Fill	Yes (default) fills the polygon with the color indicated in Center Color. Choose No to show the outline only.
Center Color	Default color depends on your hardware. Press F6 (Choices) to choose colors from a menu.
Center Pattern	0 (default—no pattern). Press F6 (Choices) to see a menu of pattern choices.

Note

See also Editing Objects, Copying an Object, and Deleting an Object.

Polylines

Purpose

A line that connects two or more points. Use Draw/ Annotate to add *polylines* to your chart. Use polyline to draw a single, straight line. You can anchor the line, you can continue drawing at a new angle, creating a zigzag effect.

Procedures

To draw with a polyline:

1. Display your chart and then press Esc until you see the Main Menu.

2. From the Main Menu, select Draw/Annotate.

3. Select Add.

4. Select Polyline.

5. Press F8 (Options) to select polyline options.

6. Press F8 (Draw) to draw the polyline.

7. Move the target to the point where you want the line to begin and press Enter.

8. Use the cursor-movement keys to move the target.

   Press Shift to force Harvard Graphics to draw the line vertically or horizontally.

   Press Backspace to rub out part of the line if you go too far.

9. To anchor the line and continue drawing another segment, press Enter. Otherwise, press Esc.

Options

You can use these Polyline options:

Color	Default color depends on your hardware. Press F6 (Choices) to see a menu of color options.
Style	Solid line (default). Choose dotted line, dashed line, or double line.
Shape	Sharp (default). Choose Curved to round off angles at polyline junctions.
Close	No (default). Choose Yes to close a polyline and form a polygon.

Note

See also Editing an Object, Copying an Object, and Deleting an Object.

═ Practice Cards ═

Purpose

One page printouts that list the order in the presentation, the file name, the description you typed when you saved the chart, and notes for your speech for each slide.

Procedures

To create and print practice cards for the current slide show:

1. From the Main Menu, select Slide Show Menu.

2. Select Make Practice Cards.

3. When the first Practice Card form appears, type your speech or comment notes for the first slide.

4. If the chart is a graph chart, select Yes at the Print Data field if you want to print the chart data when you produce output.

5. Press F10 when you finish.

6. Repeat Steps 2 through 4 until you fill out practice cards for all the slides in your show.

7. Press F10 or Esc to return to the Slide Show Menu.

8. Press Esc to return to the Main Menu.

9. Select Produce Output.

10. Select Print Practice Cards to print the charts and practice cards for the slide show.

    You see the Practice Cards Options menu.

11. If you want to print only some of the practice cards, specify the beginning card number at the From Slide field and the ending card number at the To Slide field.

    You also can choose print quality (draft, standard, or high) and select a printer (Printer 1 or 2).

12. Press F10 (Continue).

Printers

Purpose

You can use Harvard Graphics with a wide variety of printers. You can define two printers, if your system has them, or if you plan to use your data on another system that is connected to a different printer.

Procedures

To specify the printer you are using:

1. From the Main Menu, select Setup.

2. Select Printer 1.

3. Use the cursor-movement keys or the mouse to select the printer you are using.

4. When you see the Parallel/Serial overlay window, use the cursor-movement keys to highlight the port to which your printer is connected (LPT1, LPT2, COM1, COM2, or COM3).

   If you selected a serial port (one of the COM options), change the default baud rate, parity, data bits, and stop bits settings if necessary. Consult your printer's manual to determine which settings are required.

5. Press Enter.

Harvard Graphics saves the option you choose, and that option becomes the new default for the program.

To install a second printer:

Repeat these steps, but choose Printer 2 from the Setup menu.

Note

See Printing with a Printer for information on printing your charts.

Printing with a Plotter

Purpose

Prints the current chart or a slide show with your plotter.

Procedures

To print the current chart:

1. From the Main Menu, select Product Output.

2. Select Plotter.

3. Select options from the Plot Chart Options menu, if you want.

4. Press F10 (Continue) to start printing.

Options

You can choose from these Plot Chart options:

Quality	Draft (default—low resolution). Choose Standard (medium resolution) or High (high resolution).
Transparency	No (default). To draw the chart more slowly on transparency film, choose Yes.
Pause for Pen	No (default). Choose Yes if you have chosen more colors than your plotter can accommodate in its pen holders. Harvard Graphics prompts you to change pens.
Number of Copies	1 (default). Type the number of copies you want to print. **Note**: your printer must use continuous feed paper.

Note

See Slide Shows for information on printing slide shows.

Printing with a Printer

Purpose

Prints the current chart or a slide show with your plotter. If you want, you can print just the chart data.

Procedures

To print the current chart:

1. From the Main Menu, select Produce Output.

2. Select Printer.

3. Select options from the Print Chart Options menu, if you want.

4. Press **F10** (Continue) to start printing.

To print only the chart data:

1. From the Main Menu, select Produce Output.

2. Select Print Chart Data.

3. Select the destination printer (Printer 1 or 2).

4. Press **F10** (Continue) to start printing.

Options

You can choose from the following Print Chart options:

Quality   Draft (default—low resolution). Choose Standard (medium resolution) or High (high resolution).

Chart Size	Full (default). Choose 1/2 to print the chart at 50 percent size, 1/3 to print the chart at 33 percent size, or 1/4 to print the chart at 25 percent size.
Paper Size	Choose Letter (default) to print the chart on 8 1/2-by-11 inch paper. Choose Wide to print on 8 1/2-by-14-inch paper (be sure to set Chart Size to Full).
Printer	Printer 1 (default). If you installed two printers, choose Printer 2 to select the second printer.
Color	Yes (default). Choose No to print the chart in black only, using patterns instead of colors.
Number of Copies	1 (default). Type the number of copies you want to print. *Note*: your printer must use continuous feed paper.

Note

See Slide Shows for information on printing slide shows.

Quitting Harvard Graphics

Procedures

To quit the program:

1. From the Main Menu, select Exit.

If the Main Menu is not on the screen, press Esc.

2. If you see a warning that there is work you have not saved, press Esc to cancel or Enter to abandon the work you have done.

Saving a Chart

Procedures

To save a chart to disk:

1. Press Esc to return to the Main Menu.

2. Select Get/Save/Remove.

3. Select Save Chart.

4. When the Save Chart overlay appears, type a new directory name if you do not want to use the one listed at Directory.

5. Press Tab and type a file name of up to eight letters or numbers. Do not type a period or extension.

6. Press Tab and type a brief description of the chart.

7. Press F10 (Continue)

After you save your chart, you can continue working because the chart remains in memory. From the Main Menu, select Enter/Edit chart.

Scaling

Purpose

Adjusts values in the Chart Data form so that your chart reports the data truthfully. You also can use scaling to reduce visual clutter on your chart.

Procedures

To supply a scaling factor manually:

A scaling factor divides the values in a series by a factor such as 100 or 1000. Scaling factors are very useful for reducing the length of values. Therefore, scaling factors reduce the visual complexity of the chart.

So that your audience will know the scaling factor, always add a legend, such as 'Hundreds' or 'Thousands.' Harvard Graphics automatically supplies scaling factors and legends for area charts, bar/line charts, and high/low/close charts. You can change the scaling factor if you want, but if you do, you must change the legend.

The program does *not* automatically scale pie chart values. If you scale these values manually, you must add a legend manually.

1. Display the Chart Data form for the chart you want to scale.

2. Press F8 (Options)

3. If you are scaling an area chart, a bar/line chart, or a high/low/close chart, press PgDn to display Page 3 of the Titles & Options form and tab to Format.

   If you are scaling a pie chart, press PgDn to display Page 2 of the Pie Chart Titles and Options Screen and tab to Value Formats.

4. Type the scaling factor followed by a vertical line character (|).

   Common scaling factors are 100 and 1000.

To specify how many decimal places Harvard Graphics shows, type the number of decimal places after the vertical line character (**1000|2** shows the value in thousands with two decimal places).

You also can add currency symbols and other text to the values format.

5. Press **F2** (Draw) to preview the formatting.

6. Add a legend informing your audience of the scaling factor you chose.

    You can add the legend in at Footnote in the Chart Data form. If you already used the Footnote title area, you can add the legend using an annotation.

To specify the minimum and maximum y-axis values:

Harvard Graphics automatically scales the y-axis of area, bar/line, and high/low/close charts. The program always uses 0 (zero) as a minimum value to conform to well-establish principles of good graphics practice. The program also supplies y-axis increments (5, 10, 100, and so on). When the data include figures in the thousands or higher, the program uses a scaling factor and inserts a legend at the upper left corner of the frame.

You can control the y-axis manually if you want, but there is rarely reason to do so. Do not use a minimum value other than 0 (zero) because doing so falsely magnifies the data's variability. If you do, use annotation to tell your audience you used a minimum y-axis value greater than 0.

If you supply a maximum y-axis value, it will probably be greater than the one Harvard Graphics chooses automatically and will serve only to

compress the data and reduce its apparent
variability. If you are not happy with the step factor
Harvard Graphics chooses to increment the y-axis
values, you can specify a new increment:

To change the y-axis minimum, maximum, or
increment values, type a number at Minimum Value,
Maximum Value or Increment in the Titles &
Options Form.

To specify the minimum and maximum x-axis values:

If your area, bar/line, or high/low/close chart looks
cramped because too many x-axis labels are
displayed, you can reduce your chart's visual
complexity by restricting the display of x-axis items.

If you are using a calendrical, time, or numerical
x-axis data type, you can control the increment by
pressing **F3** (Set X Type) and typing an increment
factor at Increment.

Even if you chose the Name data type, however, you
can specify an increment at Increment in the Titles
& Options form.

When you specify x-axis minimum, maximum, and
increment values, you use the Pt numbers you see in
the first column of the Chart Data form.

To change the X axis minimum, maximum, or
increment values, type a Pt number at Minimum
Value, Maximum Value or Increment in the Titles &
Options Form.

Note

See also Logarithmic Charts, X Axis Data Types, and
Annotations.

Scientific Notation

Purpose

Use to reduce visual clutter when you create a chart or graph for presentation purposes If you are planning to work with very large or very small numbers, you can reduce clutter by typing such numbers in scientific notation.

Any number can be expressed several ways. For example, 100 can be expressed as 10 X 10, 1 X 100, or 1.0 X 10^3. Scientific notation expresses a number using the last of the three examples just given. The first number, which is called a *coefficient*, is multiplied by the second number, which is always 10 with an exponent. Scientific notation enables you to type a very large or very small number using just a few characters.

Procedures

To use scientific notation with Harvard Graphics:

Use the following formats:

Decimal Number	Scientific Notation	Harvard Graphics
1,000,000	1.0 X 10^6	1E6
3,560,000	3.56 X 10^6	3.56E6
0.0049	4.9 X 10^{-3}	4.9E-3
-10,000	-1.0 X 10^4	-1E-4

The positive number you enter must be between 1E20 and 1E-20, while the negative numbers you enter must be between -1E20 and -1E-20.

Screenshows

Purpose

To display a screenshow, you must first create a slideshow. You can add special effects such as erase transitions and display times. You can provide the viewer with alternative pathways through the screenshow.

Procedures

To display a screenshow from a slideshow you created:

1. From the Main Menu, select Slide Show Menu.

2. Select Select Slide Show.

3. Use the cursor-movement keys to highlight the name of the slide show you want to present.

   If you don't see the slide show file name, press F3 (Change Dir) to display other subdirectories.

4. Press Enter to choose the slide show.

5. Choose Display Screenshow.

   Harvard Graphics shows the first chart in the slideshow on the screen.

6. To display the next chart, press any key.

   Note: It takes several seconds for Harvard Graphics to respond to this command.

   To interrupt the show so you can edit a chart, press Ctrl-E.

To create a screenshow with special effects:

1. Choose Add Screenshow Effects from the Slide Show Menu.

2. When the Screenshow Effects form appears, type new default settings at Defaults if you want.

Specify defaults for Draw (controls how the chart appears on the screen), Direction (specify direction for special drawing effects), Time (controls the amount of time a chart stays on the screen), Erase (controls how the chart leaves the screen), and Dir (specify direction for special erasing techniques).

Press F6 (Choices) to see a menu of transition (drawing and erasing) and direction choices.

To choose a display time, use the standard minute:second time notation. The default time unit is seconds. If you just type 30, Harvard Graphics displays the slide for 30 seconds.

3. Select transition, time, and direction options for each chart in the show.

4. Press F10.

To provide the viewer alternative pathways through the show:

1. Create a text chart that lists the keys and alternative pathways you want to provide and make it the first chart in the show. Then add the chart to your slideshow using the editing techniques introduced in the slide show section.

   Press Ctrl-Up arrow to place the text chart at the beginning of the list of charts in the Create/ Edit Slide Show form.

2. Select Add Screenshow Effects.

3. When the Screenshow Effects form appears, place the cursor on the first chart from which you want to provide an alternative pathway.

4. Press F8 (User Menu).

   You see an overlay with two columns, Key and Go To.

5. Under the Key column, type the key you want the user to press.

   Type a number or letter.

6. Under the Go To column, type a slide number.

7. Continue naming keys and chart numbers until you finish.

8. Press **F10** (Continue)

To create a screenshow that runs continuously (until the viewer presses Esc):

1. Place the cursor in any column for the last file and press **F8**

2. Leave the key blank and type **1** in the Go To column.

Options

You can use the following special effects in your screenshow:

Blinds	Opens the screen in vertical or horizontal stripes-**R**ight and left or **U**p and down (default).
Close	Closes the screen in a vertical line in two directions simultaneously—**L**eft and right or **U**p and down (default)
Fade	Fades the existing slide off and/ or fades the new one on— **D**own or **F**ull screen fade (default)
Iris	Closes the existing screen in all directions toward the center or opens out in all directions from the center—**I**n or **O**ut (default)
Open	Opens the screen from a vertical line in two directions simultaneously—**L**eft and right or **U**p and down (default)

Overlay	Displays the slide element by element, overlaying the existing slide.
Rain	Gradually fades the screen off and/or on the screen from the top down.
Replace	Pops the new screen all at once.
Scroll	Scrolls the screen to display the new slide—**R**ight, **L**eft, **U**p (default), or **D**own.
Weave	Weaves the slide horizontally in two directions.
Wipe	Wipes the existing slide off the screen and wipes the new one on—**R**ight (default), **L**eft, **U**p, or **D**own

---

Keys

Use the following keys when creating a screenshow:

Esc	Stops the screenshow.
←	Displays the previous slide.
Backspace	Displays the previous slide.
↑	Displays the previous slide.
Home	Starts the show over
End	Displays the last slide.
Space bar	Pauses and continues displaying the current chart until any key is pressed.
Ctrl-E	Displays Chart Data form for current chart.

Note

Be sure to preview the special effects before showing
them to an audience.

═Setup Options

Purpose

After you install Harvard Graphics, you choose new
default settings for your system hardware. These settings
remain in effect unless you deliberately change them or
override them.

You choose new default settings using the Setup option
in the Main Menu.

Procedures

1. From the Main Menu, select Setup.

2. Select a new default orientation, border, and
   font for your charts; a new menu color scheme;
   a printer, plotter, and film recorder to match your
   equipment choices; the correct screen driver for
   your hardware; the default directory for storing
   your charts and template and retrieving
   spreadsheet data.

Note

See Default Settings for a list of the system defaults
as they are set when you install the program for the
first time. See also Orientation, Border, Font, Printer,
Plotter, Film Recorder, ChartBooks, Importing from
Lotus 1-2-3, and Templates.

Simple List Charts

Purpose

Includes a title in large type, an optional subtitle in smaller type, and optional footnote in the lower left corner.

Procedures

To create a bullet list text chart:

1. At the Main Menu, press F8 (Options) if you want to change the default orientation, border, and font settings for this chart.

2. From the Main Menu, select Create New Chart.

3. Select Text.

4. Select Simple List.

5. At the Title field, type a title for the chart.

6. Press Tab to move to the Subtitle field, and type a subtitle.

   The subtitle is optional. To skip it, just press Tab.

7. Press Tab to move to the Footnote field

   The footnote is optional. To skip it, just press Tab.

8. Press Tab to move to the list area.

9. Type the first item in the list.

10. Press Enter twice.

    Leave a blank line between items.

11. Type the next item in the list.

12. Repeat Steps 10 and 11 to complete the chart.

13. Press F2 (Draw Chart) to preview the chart.

If some of the lines overflow the screen, correct
the problem by using the Size/Place command.

14. Save the chart to disk.

Notes

You can change the attributes of any text on the screen.

Add visual appeal to your pie chart with symbols,
freehand illustrations, and other enhancements using
Draw/Annotate.

After you complete your chart, perform a spell check.

See also Attributes, Draw/Annotate, Size/Place, and
Spell Check.

Size/Place

Purpose

Controls the text's size and alignment (flush left,
centered, or flush right) with the Size/Place command.
You can indent text from the left on simple list and
bullet list text charts.

Procedures

To change the size of text:

1. Press F7 (Size/Place) to display size and
   alignment information next to the text areas of
   the chart.

   You see Size and Place columns on the left of
   the screen.

2. To change the text size, use the cursor-
   movement keys to highlight the size you want to
   change.

3. Type a smaller or larger size.

4. Press **F2** (Draw Chart) to make sure that none of the text lines are truncated (cut off) by the sides of the screen. Then press **Esc**.

If the text lines are truncated, use Size/Place again and choose a smaller size.

To change the alignment of text:

1. Press **F7** (Size/Place) to display size and alignment information next to the text areas of the chart.

2. To change the alignment size, use the cursor-movement keys to highlight the alignment you.

3. Type a smaller or larger size.

4. Press **F2** (Draw Chart) to make sure that none of the text lines are truncated (cut off) by the sides of the screen. Then press **Esc**.

   If the text lines are truncated, use Size/Place again and choose a smaller size.

Notes

Text sizes are not in printer's points. The sizes are relative to the font and page orientation you are using. With Landscape orientation and the Executive font, a size of 50 is about 1.50 tall, a size of 20 is about 10, and a size of 6 is about .250. You can choose any size from 1 to 99.9, including decimal fractions such as 30.5.

Slide Shows

Purpose

Create a Harvard Graphics slide show when you want to produce a desktop computer presentation (a screenshow) or create practice cards for your presentation. Once you create the slide show, you can edit the slide show form if

you want to add charts, delete charts, or change the order
of their presentation. You can print, plot, or record the
entire slide show or the slide show list.

Procedures

To create a slide show:

1. From the Main Menu, select Slide Show.

2. Select Create Slide Show.

3. When the Create/Edit Slide Show form appears,
   use the cursor-movement keys to highlight a
   chart name in the top half of the screen.

   This chart will be the first chart in the show.

4. Press Enter to select the chart.

5. Repeat Steps 4 and 5 until you choose all the
   charts you want to include in your show.

   You can include up to 90 charts.

6. Press F10.

7. To make a printed copy of the show list, select
   Produce Output from the Main Menu and then
   select Print Slide Show List.

To edit the current slide show:

1. From the Main Menu, select Slide Show.

2. Select Edit Slide Show.

3. To add a chart to the show list, place the cursor
   on its name in the top half of the window and
   press Enter.

4. To move or delete a chart from the show list,
   press Tab to move the cursor to the bottom half
   of the screen.

   *To change the order in which charts are
   displayed:*

   Place the cursor on a chart name and press Ctrl-
   Up arrow to move the chart up in the list, or
   press Ctrl-Down arrow to move the chart down.

To delete a chart from the show list:

Place the cursor on the name of the chart you want to delete and press **Ctrl-Ins**. Harvard Graphics just deletes the chart from the show list, not from disk.

5. Press **F10** (Continue).

To print a slide show with your printer, plotter, or film recorder:

1. From the Main Menu, select **S**lide Show Menu.

2. Choose **S**elect Slide Show.

3. Use the Select Slide Show form to retrieve the slide show from disk.

    Use the up- and down-arrow keys to select the slide show you want.

4. Press **F10** (Continue)

5. Press **Esc** to display the Main Menu.

6. Select **P**roduce Output.

7. Select **P**rint Slide Show, **P**lot Slide Show, and **R**ecord Slide Show.

8. When the options menu appears, choose the output options you want. If you do not want to print, plot, or record the entire slide show, type the number of the beginning slide at the From Slide field and the ending slide at the To Slide field. Choose **Y**es at the Collate field if you want to produce collated multiple copies of the slide show.

9. Press **F10** (Continue).

To print the current slide show list:

1. From the Main Menu, select **P**roduce Output.

2. Select **P**rint Slide Show List.

3. Select a printer (Printer 1 or 2), if desired.

4. Press **F10** (Continue).

Note

See also Screenshow and Practice Cards.

Spell Check ════════════════════════

Purpose

Check your spelling every time you complete a chart.
Spelling errors send the wrong message about you and
your organization. Thanks to the Harvard Graphics F4
(Spell Check) key, this task is now virtually automatic.
In addition to spelling errors, Spell Check detects
improper capitalization (cAlifornia), improper number
punctuation ($50,00.00), improper punctuation
(!widgets), and repeated words (the the).

Like all computer spelling checkers, Harvard Graphic's
spell checker questions properly spelled words that are
not in its dictionary, such as proper nouns. Fortunately,
you can add correctly spelled words to the Harvard
Graphics dictionary so that these words will not be
flagged in future spell checking sessions.

Procedures

To check the spelling on any Harvard Graphics chart:

1. After creating your chart, press Esc to return to
   the Main Menu.

   Your chart remains in memory.

2. Press F4 (Spell Check).

   If Spell Check finds a word on your chart that it
   cannot match with the words in its dictionary,
   you see the message Word Not In
   Dictionary. Spell Check also attempts to
   find likely correct spellings of the word. If any
   such spellings are found, they are displayed at
   the bottom of the Spell Check window.

3. If the word is correctly spelled and you do not want to add it to the dictionary, choose Word OK, continue and press Enter.

   If the word is correctly spelled and you *do* want to add it to the dictionary, choose Add to Dictionary.

   If the word is misspelled and you see the correct spelling at the bottom of the window, use the cursor-movement keys to highlight the correct spelling and press Enter.

   If the word is misspelled and you do not see the correct spelling at the bottom of the window, choose Type Correction. Type the correct spelling, and press Enter.

4. When you see the message `Spell check complete,` press Enter to continue.

To quit Spell Check at any time:

Press **Esc**.

Harvard Graphics makes all the changes you requested up to the point you pressed Esc.

Stacked Bar Charts

Purpose

A variation on bar/line charts, stacked bar charts place data series on top of one another. For this reason, they produce a multicolored or multipatterned bar for each x-axis category. This bar dramatically conveys the idea that each bar represents components of a whole.

Procedures

To create a stacked bar chart:

1. Follow the instructions for bar/line charts to enter the data.

2. Press F8 (Options).

3. Press PgDn and select Stack at the Bar Style field.

4. Press F2 (Draw) to preview your chart.

Starting Harvard Graphics

Purpose

Starting Harvard Graphics is a simple matter once you install the program. If you have not installed Harvard Graphics, read Installing Harvard Graphics before proceeding.

Procedures

To start the program on a hard disk system:

1. Type CD C:\HGDATA to change to the Harvard Graphics data directory.

2. Type C:\HG and press Enter.

   If you see the message Bad command or file name, make sure that the statement PATH C:\HG is in your AUTOEXEC.BAT file.

To start the program on a system with two 3 1/2-inch disk drives:

1. Insert your working copy of the Harvard Graphics Program disk in drive A.

2. Insert your working chart disk in drive B.

3. Make drive B the default drive by typing B:\ and pressing Enter.

4. At the B> prompt, type HG and press Enter.

Because you started Harvard Graphics from the data directory, the program automatically uses this directory for storing the charts you create.

Symbols

Purpose

Use Draw/Annotate to include more than 200 symbols in your Harvard Graphics charts and graphs.

Procedures

To include a symbol in your graph:

1. Make the chart you want to modify the current chart.

2. Press Esc to display the Main Menu.

3. Select Draw/Annotate.

4. Select Symbol.

5. Select Get.

6. When the Select Symbol File form appears, use the up- or down-arrow keys to choose a symbol file.

7. Move the target to the symbol you want and press Enter.

8. Move the corner of the box marked by the target to enlarge or reduce the symbol

   Hold down the Shift key as you move the target to preserve the proportions of the symbol.

9. Press Enter.

10. To move the symbol where you want it to appear on your chart, press Backspace.

11. Move the target to the place you want the symbol's upper left corner to appear, and press Enter.

12. Move the target to the place you want the symbol's lower left corner to appear, and press Enter.

To preserve the symbol's proportions, hold down
the Shift key as you use the cursor-movement
keys to move the symbol.

13. Press **F10** (Continue).

Templates

Purpose

Enables you to use an existing chart as a pattern from
which you construct new charts. When you create a
chart, you invest a lot of time in choosing colors,
attributes, fonts, and other options so that the chart
conforms to your tastes and needs. Instead of
reinventing the wheel next time you create a chart, use
an existing chart as a template.

Procedures

To create a template:

1. Create or retrieve a text chart, an organization
   chart, or a graph chart with the options you want.

2. Press **Esc** to return to the Main Menu.

3. Select **Get/Save/Remove**.

4. Select **Save Template**.

5. When the Save Template menu appears, use one
   of the predefined template names.

6. Select **Yes** to clear the values.

   Harvard Graphics retains the attributes, text size
   and placement, current chart options (the ones
   you chose after you pressed **F8**), and
   annotations.

7. Press **F10** to create the template.

After you create the template, add it to a chartbook.

Use the following guide to template names:

Area charts	Area
Bar/Line charts	Barline
Bullet list charts	Bullet
Free form charts	Freeform
High/Low/Close charts	HLC
Multiple charts	Multiple
Organization charts	Org
Pie charts	Pie
Simple list charts	List
Three-column charts	3_Column
Title charts	Title
Two-column charts	2_Column

Text Charts

Purpose

Text charts are frequently used as an accompaniment to an oral presentation. An effective text chart conveys unified information using familiar, concise words. You can choose from five text chart formats:

Title Chart	Ideal for the opening of a presentation or handout. The title chart workscreen provides areas for three lines of text: a large, main title, a smaller subtitle, and a second subtitle. Each line is centered.
Free Form Text Chart	If you want to control how the text is aligned by positioning words manually,

choose a free form chart. If you prefer to have Harvard Graphics align the text automatically, however, choose a simple list or bullet list chart.

Simple List Chart

Useful for identifying the main subjects of a presentation. Simple lists have a large, centered title at the top, followed by a subtitle. The items in the list are centered. You can place a footnote in the lower left corner.

Bullet List Chart

Each item is preceded by a bullet symbol, such as a dot, a square, or a check mark. The items are aligned left flush.

Column Text Chart

Shows information in two or three vertical columns below the title. Use this format to display a few numbers, such as sales totals from three departments.

If you have much numerical information to convey, and especially if you want to convey the relationships within this information, you may prefer to create a bar/line chart.

Note

For information on creating these text charts, see Bullet List Charts, Column Text Charts, Free Form Text Charts, Simple List Charts, and Title Text Charts.

Title Charts

Purpose

Use to open your presentation or handout. You can place up to 60 characters on each line. The best title charts, however, have 30 characters or fewer on a line.

The title chart is divided into three text areas (Top, Middle, and Bottom). You can place three lines in each area. By default, each line is centered. You can choose other alignment using the Size/Place command.

Procedures

To create a title chart:

1. At the Main Menu, press F8 (Options) to change the default orientation, border, and font settings for this chart.

2. Select Create New Chart.

3. Select Text.

4. Select Title Chart.

5. In the Top text area, type the main title.

   This title appears in large type.

6. In the Middle text area, type the first subtitle.

   The subtitle appears in smaller type.

7. In the Bottom text area, type the second subtitle, if desired.

   This subtitle appears in the smallest type.

8. Press F10 (Continue).

9. Type the first item in the list.

10. Press Enter twice.

11. Type the next item in the list.

12. Repeat Steps 14 and 15 to complete the chart.

13. Press **F2** (Draw Chart) to preview the chart.

    If some of the lines overflow the screen, correct the problem by using the Size/Place command.

14. Save the chart to disk.

Notes

You can change the attributes of any text on the screen.

Add visual appeal to your pie chart with symbols, freehand illustrations, and other enhancements using Draw/Annotate.

After you complete your chart, perform a spell check.

See also Attributes, Draw/Annotate, Size/Place, and Spell Check.

Trend Line Charts

Purpose

A line chart in which the individual data points are not necessarily connected by the line. Instead, Harvard Graphics calculates a line of best fit to show the overall trend represented by the data points.

You can choose from five different types of trend lines: linear, exponential regression, linear regression, logarithmic regression, and power regression.

Procedures

To create a linear trend line chart:

1. Press **F8** (Options).

2. At the Type field, choose Trend for each data series.

3. To create the other trend line charts, you perform a calculation on a data series to produce and display a new, calculated data series.

Note

See also Calculation.

Two Pie/Column Charts

Purpose

Displays two pie charts, two column charts, or one pie chart and one column chart on the same screen. In this section, you learn how to display two pie or column charts.

Although you can display only two pie charts at a time, you can add up to eight data series to each Pie Chart Data form. If you create more than two data series, you can choose which two data series to display as Pie 1 and Pie 2.

Procedures

To create a two pie/column chart:

1. Create the first pie or column chart following the instructions in Pie Charts or Column Charts.

2. Press **PgDn** to display Page 2 of the Pie Chart Data form.

   Use this form to enter the labels. You see the message `Pie Chart 2 Data, Page 2 of 20` at the top of the screen. Under Values, you see Series 2.

   If you want to create additional data series, press **F9** (More Series) and add another set of labels and values.

3. Type the labels and values of the second pie or column chart.

4. Press F8 (Options).

5. Press Tab to go to the Pie 1 Title and type a title for Pie 1.

6. Press Tab to go to the Pie 2 Title and type a title for Pie 2.

7. Press F2 to preview your chart.

8. Save the chart to disk.

Notes

Select **Y**es at the Proportional Pies field in the Pie Chart Titles & Options form to display the pies in sizes proportional to their values.

If you created more than two data series, press PgUp to display Page 1 of the Pie Chart Data form. Then press F9 (More Series) to display the data series you want to appear as Pie 1. (The next series in the sequence will be displayed as Pie 2.)

You can change a two pie/column chart to a bar line chart, but only if the labels in both pies match. The reason is that Harvard Graphics converts the Pie 1 labels into x-axis categories. The Pie 2 labels will be lost. If the Pie 2 labels do not match the Pie 1 labels, the Pie 2 data will not make any sense when graphed against the new x-axis categories.

To change the size and position of Pie 1 and Pie 2 titles, display Page 1 of the Pie Chart Titles & Options form and press F7 (Size/Place). You can place the titles above or below the pie.

To change the attributes of the Pie 1 and Pie 2 titles, display Page 1 of the Pie Chart Titles & Options form and press F7 (Size/Place).

For information on linking the two so that the second chart breaks down the components of a slice, see Linked Pie/Column Charts. See also Pie Charts, Column Charts, and Pie Chart Titles & Options.

Value Formats

Purpose

Controls the way Harvard Graphics displays values, you
can type a format instruction. Even if you choose the
Currency option, you must use a format instruction if
you want Harvard Graphics to display values with
commas and two decimal points.

Procedures

To enter value formats for a bar/line chart:

1. Press **F8** (Options) to display the Bar/Line Chart
   Titles & Options form.

2. Press **PgDn** to display Page 3.

3. Press **Tab** to go to the Format field and type the
   format instruction in the Y1 Axis column.

To enter value formats for a pie chart:

1. Press **F8** (Options) to display the Pie Chart Titles
   & Options form.

2. Press **PgDn** to display Page 2.

3. Press **Tab** to go to the Value Format field and
   type the format instruction.

Notes

You can type more than one format instruction.

To display currency values with two decimal points and
commas, type ,2 when you enter the format instruction.

Format	Purpose
, (comma)	Displays values with commas.
Number from 0 to 9	Specifies number of decimal places to display.

Text		Displays the text before all values.
	Text	Displays the text after all values.
	!	Displays number with scientific notation.

X Axis Data Types

Purpose

When you create a bar/line chart, you may take advantage of a convenient Harvard Graphics feature that automates the entry of calendrical, time, and numerical categories along the x-axis. If you do not want to take advantage of this feature, just choose the Name option on the X Data Type Menu.

Procedure

If you choose any other option besides Name in this menu, you must make an entry at the Starting With and Ending With fields. No entry is required at Increment unless you want to change the default increment (1).

Note

For most data types, you choose from several alternative formats, and Harvard Graphics echoes your choice when it adds the items to the x-axis column. For example, if you type January at the Starting With field, the program places January, February, March, and so on, in the x-axis column. However, if you type JAN at the Starting With field, you see JAN, FEB, MAR, and so on in the x-axis column.

Index